Volume 1

iPhone
Apps Book

The Essential Directory of iPhone & iPod Touch Applications

Prima Games
An Imprint of Random House, Inc.
3000 Lava Ridge Court, Suite 100
Roseville, CA 95661
www.primagames.com

Senior Product Manager: Mario De Govia
Associate Product Manager: Shaida Boroumand
Design & Layout: Mojo Media

Content packaged by:
mojo-media.com
Joe Funk, Editor
Jason Hinman, Creative Director

Important
Prima Games has made every effort to determine that the information
contained in this book is accurate. However, the publisher makes no
warranty, either expressed or implied, as to the accuracy, effectiveness,
or completeness of the material in this book; nor does the publisher assume
liability for damages, either incidental or consequential, that may result
from using the information in this book. The publisher cannot provide any
additional information or support regarding gameplay, hints and strategies,
or problems with hardware or software. Such questions should be directed
to the support numbers provided by the game and/or device manufacturers
as set forth in their documentation. Some game tricks require precise timing
and may require repeated attempts before the desired result is achieved.

ISBN: 978-0-7615-6285-6
Library of Congress Control Number: 2009908294
Printed in the United States of America
09 10 11 12 GG 10 9 8 7 6 5 4 3 2 1

Contents

To Sharon, Joey & Janey—my never ending
sources of inspiration.

Introduction

One Giant Leap···

Ever since PCs came on the scene, I've been a bit of a technology geek. In fact, my first computer was an Apple II+ with 48K and being the techie as I was, even in junior high school, I upgraded the RAM 16K to expand it to a kickin' 64K!

Since then, I've remained what has become known as an early adopter—one of those people who has to have the latest in technology—though along the way, as my life has gone on and other priorities have popped up, the latest in technology has become much more widely available to the masses. You don't need to drive to that specialty computer store or audio boutique any more, for now you can get admirably performing electronics at big box stores.

Fast-forward to 2007, and being the techie that I still am (albeit now with young kids in tow), I was watching the latest portable DVD players shrink in size and scale in the 2000s—you know the kind you can bring on an airplane or train, or throw on the kid's lap during a long drive. I was zeroing in on the latest Sony when Apple released the iPhone and iPod Touch in September 2007.

Cell phones had already been around for three decades. DVD players had been around for 10 years, but it struck me at the time, and it still does now, that this wasn't your typical incremental step in technology, this was a 5-10 year, giant leap forward in evolution. Apple, representing the best of modern American innovation and business savvy, blew the screens off the competition and delivered one of the first truly revolutionary products of the new millennium.

And it wasn't just the small but mighty hardware. The brilliantly simple and intuitive user interface Apple developed for iTunes became even more functional and flexible when the touch screen came into play. Finally, no more keeping that hard-to-find, obtusely-translated user guide nearby to remember what all those buttons do. Everyone from 6-year-olds to 66-year-olds can navigate through an iPhone or iPod touch the moment it's placed in their hands.

In fact, the Apple user interface and hardware combination is so revolutionary that we have a long way to go before the masses grasp how life-changing it is. This cannot be overstated. Even most heavy users of the iPhone and iPod touch don't realize how deep and dynamic this exploding library of content is going to be.

iTunes changed forever the way we looked at, and listened to, our music libraries. The iPhone will forever change the way we use the internet, consume data and watch video. From micro-transactions to the ability to recognize where you are in the world at any given moment, we've still only scratched the surface of how useful this amazing device will become in our modern, mobile lives.

—Joe Funk, September 2009

How To Use This Book

Yes, we know there are new Apps coming out every day.

Yes, we know there are more than 10,000 Apps already available and the library is growing exponentially.

In fact, the speed and volume with which new Apps are launching is the strength of this book. It serves as a time stamp to highlight the latest greatest Apps, including stuff you may have already missed in the avalanche of new releases.

This book is basically the "Best of" everything that has come out so far according to our editorial panel, right up to our print date in Fall 2009. It is broken down into the same main categories (1) that Apple breaks the Apps into in the iTunes store, so you should be able to find what you're interested in via our thumb tabs quickly and conveniently. At the end of each chapter is the snappily-named Apps Capsules, which is a last, dense grouping of Apps in each category that we felt deserved honorable mention.

For each App, we include obligatory info such as the creator, pricing and release date (2); a summary of the App (3); an explanation of why we chose it (3); and in some cases we include an extra blurb or factoid on something related to the App (4). We also include a few screen shots of the App (5).

Whether you are already an addict or a new user of the iPhone or iPod Touch, or know someone who has just joined the Apple army and is looking for some quick, solid additions to fill a barren screen, we are confident you'll find this book handy.

1. Category

Quick Review

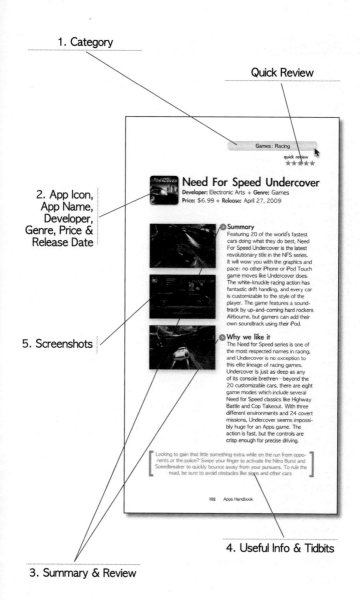

Games: Racing

quick review
★★★★★

Need For Speed Undercover
Developer: Electronic Arts ✦ **Genre:** Games
Price: $6.99 ✦ **Release:** April 27, 2009

2. App Icon,
App Name,
Developer,
Genre, Price &
Release Date

Summary
Featuring 20 of the world's fastest cars doing what they do best, Need For Speed Undercover is the latest revolutionary title in the NFS series. It will wow you with the graphics and pace: no other iPhone or iPod Touch game moves like Undercover does. The white-knuckle racing action has fantastic drift handling, and every car is customizable to the style of the player. The game features a soundtrack by up-and-coming hard rockers Airbourne, but gamers can add their own soundtrack using their iPod.

5. Screenshots

Why we like it
The Need for Speed series is one of the most respected names in racing, and Undercover is no exception to this elite lineage of racing games. Undercover is just as deep as any of its console brethren—beyond the 20 customizable cars, there are eight game modes which include several Need for Speed classics like Highway Battle and Cop Takeout. With three different environments and 24 covert missions, Undercover seems impossibly huge for an Apps game. The action is fast, but the controls are crisp enough for precise driving.

Looking to gain that little something extra while on the run from opponents or the police? Swipe your finger to activate the Nitro Burst and Speedbreaker to quickly bounce away from your pursuers. To rule the road, be sure to avoid obstacles like signs and other cars.

102 Apps Handbook

4. Useful Info & Tidbits

3. Summary & Review

Audiobooks

Developer: Cross Forward Consulting, LLC
Genre: Books + **Price:** FREE + **Release:** May 22, 2009

❯ Summary

With access to over 1,800 audio books, the Audiobooks App is the premier solution in the App Store for listening to classics on the go. Currently with more than 10,000 hours of content thanks to access to the Librivox Project's work, Audiobooks is constantly expanding its offerings. The interface is simple and easy to use—just select an audio book from the thousands of titles available, hit download, and you're ready to go.

❯ Why we like it

While reading is an important part of daily life, there are times where it's just not convenient to open a book or even scan through an e-book. If you're stuck riding in traffic, trying to meditate, or otherwise don't have the ability to take your eyes and focus on your iPhone or iPod Touch, Audiobooks is the answer for you. Automatic bookmarking to keep your place is a handy feature that lets you stop playing and resume exactly where you left off. Quick Start Listening is also a nifty feature—instead of having to wait for the entire audio book to download, you can start listening as soon as the first chapter downloads.

3 1833 05769 6608

[The App is quite handy for people on the go, and the dedication of the team working on it is great. Where other Apps charge for less, the folks behind Audiobooks are constantly improving their product yet never charge for such terrific service.]

quick review
★★★☆☆

Kindle For iPhone

Developer: Amazon.com **+ Genre:** Books
Price: FREE **+ Release:** March 4, 2009

Summary

If you've tried other e-book readers in the past but were left unsatisfied, then Amazon's Kindle might be the reader for you. Based on the stand-alone device that has taken the e-book world by storm, Kindle For iPhone is a revolutionary new reader that has top-notch features and the power of the Amazon book library behind it. With low prices on everything from classics to new releases and New York Times Best Sellers, you're sure to find something you'd want to read from the world's biggest online book retailer.

Why we like it

If you already have an Amazon Kindle for your reading on the go, Kindle For iPhone is still a great App to get. Using Amazon's Whisper-sync technology, you can switch your library back and forth for free with no hassle at all—Kindle and Kindle For iPhone even bookmark your page so you don't lose your place in any book you're reading. One-touch downloading is a bonus. Once your account info is entered into Kindle For iPhone, the App lets you download new books with just one click.

Not sure if you want to buy a book just yet? Check out the Amazon store's free preview of every book in its library. You can read the first few pages and sometimes even the entire first chapter of a book, so you can try before you buy.

Shortcovers

Developer: Indigo Books and Music, Inc
Genre: Books + **Price:** FREE + **Release:** March 3, 2009

> Summary

A sleek and attractive e-book reader with access to a huge library of novels, short stories and magazines, Shortcovers places its outstanding content at the forefront of the App. You can search for your favorite reads like in other e-book readers, but the editors of Shortcovers want to make their service something more. They will hook you up with all the latest literary hotness and with can't-miss titles from the newest up-and-coming authors. All your favorite classics are there too: from the oldest works in literature through current New York Times Best Sellers.

> Why we like it

While Shortcovers does do books as well as any other e-book reader on the iPhone or iPod Touch, its special focus on shorter publications makes it noteworthy. Shortcovers' editors are always on the prowl for new blog posts, short stories, and magazine articles that readers may be interested in, and provides them free of charge to their readers. The ability to read the first chapter of a book is also always welcome.

[Have so much to read that you're having trouble sorting and searching it all? Organize your books, articles and speeches all relating to a certain topic or by author or any other criteria using Shortcovers' Favorite Themes list.]

quick review
★★★☆☆

Stanza

Developer: Lexcycle **+ Genre:** Books
Price: FREE **+ Release:** March 5, 2009

Summary

Looking for an alternative e-book reader that's simple to operate, doesn't take up much space and is easy on the eyes? Take a look at Stanza, one of the most popular e-book readers in the App Store. Stanza has over 100,000 titles available, including 50,000 titles for sale in the Fictionwise eReader Store and another 50,000 classics and recent titles from various free services. Stanza has been recognized by several major media outlets for its ease of use and sheer access to titles. All the big names are here, from Homer to Dan Brown and from William Shakespeare to Erik Larson.

Why we like it

If you're looking at an alternative to Amazon's Kindle For iPhone, Stanza is the best option. It has the backing of one of the largest e-book stores on the internet and has rightfully earned praise for its ease of use. Downloading new titles is a snap, and though it's not quite the one-touch downloading from Kindle, some users prefer having a few safety steps in between so they don't purchase a title accidentally. Stanza is one of the easiest book Apps to operate, with clear and precise instructions on how to get to reading. Portrait and landscape reading is also a plus.

Have other e-books you're looking to add from your PC to Stanza? The App makes it easy to download your books as Stanza supports many major formats including occasionally temperamental PDFs.

Apps Capsules

> Classics

Developer: Andrew Kaz & Phill Ryu + **Genre:** Books
Price: $0.99 + **Release:** January 3, 2009

Featuring a collection of nearly two dozen classic novels plus Homer's epic Illiad, Classics is a bargain at a buck. Promising free updates with even more books and including a fantastic reader, Classics is worth a look.

> Shakespeare

Developer: Readdle + **Genre:** Books
Price: FREE + **Release:** February 22, 2009

Featuring the complete works of Shakespeare plus some of his questionable works, Shakespeare offers a ton of content for free. Everything is completely searchable and the App offers landscape reading.

> BookZ

Developer: Steve's Studio + **Genre:** Books
Price: FREE + **Release:** May 1, 2009

Entirely free of ads or other annoyances, BookZ is a simple way to read books that are in .txt format. It features full text search, changeable fonts, and everything else you need in a full-featured reader.

> iPhone: The Missing Manual

Developer: Lexcycle + **Genre:** Books
Price: $4.99 + **Release:** November 4, 2008

The manual that should have come in the box! iPhone: The Missing Manual covers everything you need to know about your device and uncovers some secrets that may surprise you.

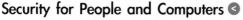
Security for People and Computers

Developer: AppEngines ♦ **Genre:** Books
Price: FREE ♦ **Release:** August 3, 2008

Featuring advice on how to make life more secure
in both the real world and in the digital realm,
Security for People and Computers offers advice
that many of us can begin using ASAP.

iRiddles!

Developer: D. Noel Keshwar ♦ **Genre:** Books
Price: $1.99 ♦ **Release:** October 28, 2008

This is a collection of mind-bending riddles that the
young and old alike will enjoy. The many types of
riddles in this App are sure to help pass your time,
and you can simply shake for a random riddle!

Wattpad

Developer: WP Technology, Inc. ♦ **Genre:** Books
Price: FREE ♦ **Release:** April 28, 2009

A giant community of readers use Wattpad and
submit content for the App, but that's not the best
part. With use of the reader, you have access to
over 100,000 free e-books!

Tips & Tricks—iPhone Secrets Lite

Developer: Intelligenti Publishing ♦ **Genre:** Books
Price: FREE ♦ **Release:** May 17, 2009

The free version of the popular Tips & Tricks book,
iPhone Secrets Lite contains the five most popular
tips from the full version. Learn some of these
helpful hints and you're on your way to becoming
a power user.

FedEx Mobile for iPhone

Developer: FedEx **+ Genre:** Business
Price: FREE **+ Release:** May 5, 2009

❯ Summary

Need up-to-date package tracking information? Have so many items in transit you
can barely follow them all? You need FedEx
Mobile for iPhone, a powerful App that brings
nearly every service available from FedEx
right to the palm of your hand. Want to know
when a package is arriving? Track it every
step of the way. Use FedEx Ship Manager to
keep tabs on packages you've sent out, and
manage your packages in sync with either
FedEx on the web or FedEx Desktop.

❯ Why we like it

Nicknaming packages and events is incredibly
handy and useful, especially when you have
two similar packages in transit that might
otherwise be easily confused by just looking
at the tracking numbers. FedEx Mobile for
iPhone is not watered down in any way—it's
great for small business owners because it
enables you to do it all, including make labels
and ship directly from your phone. While this
functionality may seem complicated, FedEx
has made it a sleek and easy-to-use package,
so if you just want to track a few packages
FedEx Mobile is the right App for you, too.

Looking to walk into a standalone store to make a shipment or conduct
other business you just can't or don't want to do with your iPhone? Use
FedEx Mobile to find any FedEx Office Print & Ship Centers, authorized
FedEx shipping locations, or FedEx Express boxes near you.

quick review
★★★☆☆

iTalk Recorder

Developer: Griffin Technology + **Genre:** Business
Price: FREE + **Release:** October 13, 2008

Summary

Are you serious about recording your thoughts, conversations, or just the sounds of the world around you? Want an App that serves as a personal voice recorder and so much more, yet is still easy to use? Look no further than iTalk Recorder. With one-touch recording, a simple interface that lets you record in three different quality modes, iTalk is a slick combination of form and function. You can even add text to your recordings to give them added context later!

Why we like it

Musicians, authors and other creative types have flocked to iTalk Recorder because it offers them something they always wish they had: a personal voice recorder ready to record thoughts and ideas at a moment's notice. You'll be surprised at how often you'll use this App, and wonder how you let so many ideas slip away for so long. Having software available to sync to a computer over WiFi is a handy option that's simple to use.

quick review
★★★☆☆

Salesforce Mobile

Developer: salesforce.com ✦ **Genre:** Business
Price: FREE ✦ **Release:** January 14, 2009

> Summary

Free for all business users of Salesforce, some of the top business software in the world today, Salesforce Mobile is a leader in its own right among its business App brethren thanks to a handy interface and powerful tools that place the functionality of your desktop in the palm of your hand. The premier software for a sales team on the go, Salesforce allows you to keep track of all your sales or service activity without having to fire up that suddenly burdensome laptop when you're on the road.

> Why we like it

Salesforce is an incredibly common business application for outside salespeople and their supervisors because it's easy to use and offers powerful functionality for staying on top of work and keeping customer wants and needs straight. The App blends in seamlessly with the desktop software and all the key functions are editable—from Opportunities to Accounts to Leads. Interested in trying out Salesforce full time based on the functionality of the App but not sure if you're ready to take the plunge? Use the App to access a free trial of the software.

[With every update, Salesforce is getting new functionality in its free App, meaning that there's increasingly less of a need to use your main computer to enter info. The newest edition features a handy clone feature which allows you to copy info and use it again.]

quick review
★★★☆☆

Documents To Go

Developer: DataViz, Inc. + **Genre:** Business
Price: $9.99 + **Release:** May 25, 2009

Business

Summary ◁

Do you simply have to have access to Microsoft's Office for your business applications with no way around it? Wish the iPhone had better access to the files you need to use and had access to your Exchange Server so you could receive all your work e-mail? Look no further than Documents To Go, an App so spectacularly convenient, you'll wonder how you lived without it. You can edit, create and view files in all popular Office formats, including Word and Excel; synchronize your files with any number of other services, including Apple's iWork; and synchronize your files two ways thanks to a handy desktop application.

Why we like it ◁

The updates being made to this App make it better all the time, and with the support level it has, it's no wonder that this is one of the best-selling Apps available. If you're a businessperson or use your iPhone for business applications, you simply must have Documents To Go. New features include support for document attachments in popular Microsoft formats when accessing your e-mail over an Exchange Server. DataViz has been adding Office functions for mobile devices for 10 years now, and they're the best at it.

[Not a business user? You can still find great features in Documents To Go. Writing a great book, school project, or creating a contract? You can work on it in Documents To Go and save it in both new and old Microsoft Word formats.]

Jobs

Developer: CareerBuilder.com + **Genre:** Business
Price: FREE + **Release:** July 9, 2008

❯ Summary

Looking for a new opportunity after losing your job? Thinking about starting down a new career path after becoming stuck in a rut? Searching for that first big break after graduating college? Let your iPhone or iPod Touch help you find that perfect career opportunity with Jobs, the free App from CareerBuilder.com. With over two million jobs all over the United States, CareerBuilder.com is one of the leading names in job hunting. Search for work using keywords, read descriptions and save to your favorites, or e-mail listings to yourself or colleagues.

❯ Why we like it

CareerBuilder.com is a useful site on its own, but it really shines when taking advantage of the iPhone's capabilities. Out in a new city looking for your next opportunity? Use the geo-location function of your device to search for gigs only in the area you're standing in. CareerBuilder.com integrates beautifully with Google Maps by also displaying a map of the city a job is placed in, which gets even more precise if an employer has added an address. For a free App, there's a ton of features here, so don't pass up the chance to find your dream job.

[
When you're browsing job descriptions along the bottom of the screen there are only two options: Search and Favorites. One feature that would be nice to see added in the future is the ability to apply for jobs straight from your iPhone.
]

quick review
★★★☆☆

Mocha VNC Lite

Developer: MochaSoft + **Genre:** Business
Price: FREE + **Release:** July 7, 2008

Summary

Looking for access to your VNC server from pretty much anywhere? Never get left in the dark again when looking for your files and folders with Mocha VNC Lite. Don't let the name and price fool you: this is a Swiss Army knife of Apps that packs a ton of features into a small package. Find your files, programs and resources just like you would on your home or work computer and seamlessly access them from your iPhone or iPod Touch.

Why we like it

Mocha VNC Lite has some great developers behind it and they've tested the software against nearly every major VNC protocol for both Windows and Mac. Featuring encrypted password sign in, security is worry-free when going back to access your file. If you're having trouble accessing your VNC server with Mocha, there are several configuration options available, including the option for six different Host configurations. For a free App, Mocha VNC Lite is very powerful; most users may never need to use the full version.

[The paid version of Mocha VNC is a great App, but not everyone needs all of its functionality. Bonus features for the full version include extra keyboard buttons, including ALT, CTRL, and the Apple button; support for a right mouse button; and a whole new keyboard option.]

FTP On the Go

Developer: Headlight Software, Inc. **+ Genre:** Business
Price: $6.99 **+ Release:** June 2, 2009

> ### Summary
The top FTP App for your iPhone and iPod Touch, FTP On the Go makes accessing your files and folders a snap. You can browse, upload and download anything in your FTP, including downloading, editing, and re-uploading files on the go. FTP On the Go has a remarkably simple interface—all you need to know are the login credentials for your FTP server, and you're good to go. With a built-in web browser and a text editor meshed into the App, there's more functionality here than in any other FTP App.

> ### Why we like it
It's nice to not always have to download a file from the FTP, exit the program, and go hunt it down. Several file types are supported to view on the fly, including most Microsoft Office files and images and videos. FTP On the Go also has a great website if you're not sure you're ready to take the plunge. It even features tutorial videos that show you how to get the most out of the App. With the iPhone's OS 3 installed, the ability to e-mail a file from your FTP to a colleague is a welcome feature.

[
FTP On the Go takes your security seriously. If you decide to save your login credentials so you don't have to enter them by hand every time you use the App, FTP On the Go allows you to set a master password no one can access if your device falls into the wrong hands.
]

quick review
★★★★☆

NearBuy Real Estate Search

Developer: NearBuy + **Genre:** Business
Price: FREE + **Release:** March 19, 2009

Business

Summary ◀

Looking for a new apartment or home to rent or purchase? Finding places for sale or rent has never been simpler than with NearBuy Real Estate Search. A comprehensive listing of places for sale in major metropolitan areas of the United States, NearBuy uses your device's location awareness features to search for the perfect place for you. It features apartments, condos, even houses, and many places even have links so you can take a virtual tour of the place—all without leaving to go look at it or calling an agent.

Why we like it ◀

The convenience is fantastic for people looking to narrow down their search for a new home without having to hit the streets and do a lot of leg work. Because it pinpoints places to live on a map, you can easily scroll around and see how far away you are from things like parks, schools, highways and public transportation. Connected to several national real estate databases, NearBuy is a powerful, full-service listing tool.

Apps Capsules

❯ ZIP Finder

Developer: Bottle Rocket ✦ **Genre:** Business
Price: FREE ✦ **Release:** December 16, 2008

Instantly find the ZIP code for wherever you are in America, Canada or Puerto Rico, and make your searches more efficient. You can also punch in a ZIP code and find out where it is in these locations.

❯ Accept Credit Cards

Developer: MerchantWarehouse.com, Inc.
Genre: Business ✦ **Price:** FREE
Release: May 15, 2009

Run credit cards through your device using this free and easy to use terminal application. All transactions, including sales, returns, and voids are secure, and the App can be used anywhere your device can connect to the internet.

❯ VehiCal—Car Expense Management

Developer: Red Cube ✦ **Genre:** Business
Price: FREE ✦ **Release:** November 30, 2008

Record and calculate just how much you're spending on your car with VehiCal. Track your vehicle's fuel consumption and average price you pay for gas. Maximize your tax deductions by tracking your business driving accurately to the last mile.

❯ Fuze Meeting

Developer: CallWave ✦ **Genre:** Business
Price: FREE ✦ **Release:** February 23, 2009

A full-featured business meeting App, Fuze Meeting allows you to conduct meetings in real time. View screen sharing and even HD video and use Fuze's web service for even more features.

To-Do List

Developer: Concrete Software, Inc **+ Genre:** Business
Price: $2.99 **+ Release:** June 15, 2009

The newest version of To-Do List packs great features into a small package. Keep track of all your lists, from work to grocery lists, in this powerful App. Sort by different categories and e-mail your tasks.

Timewerks: Mobile Billing

Developer: Sorth, LLC **+ Genre:** Business
Price: $9.99 **+ Release:** May 9, 2009

A full-featured invoicing program, Timewerks is a must-have for independent contractors and any person who needs to record their time and materials and then send invoices. Track multiple projects and clients with this full version.

Whack Pack

Developer: Creative Think **+ Genre:** Business
Price: $2.99 **+ Release:** May 9, 2009

A premier creativity tool and mind-jogger, the Creative Whack Pack forces your mind to start thinking about projects and problems in a new light. Based on the original card deck, this App will jump-start your productivity.

My Eyes Only

Developer: Software Ops, LLC **+ Genre:** Business
Price: $5.99 **+ Release:** May 29, 2009

Safely store personal information like logins, passwords, credit card information and bank account information. My Eyes Only has incredibly tight encryption measures and none of your information is ever sent to an outside server.

quick review
★★★☆☆

Wheels on the Bus

Developer: Duck Duck Moose + **Genre:** Education
Price: $0.99 + **Release:** February 11, 2009

▶ Summary

Designed by parents, for parents and their children, Wheels on the Bus has everything an App should when it comes to capturing the hearts and minds of children. With fun, beautifully designed graphics, cool sound effects and music, and great interactivity, this App will keep kids smiling for hours. An interactive musical book based on the App's namesake song, Wheels on the Bus, lets kids spin the wheel, open and shut the door, pop bubbles, move the wipers, and do much, much more. It even lets your child record his or her singing to play back later.

▶ Why we like it

Anything that can captivate kids for $0.99 is worth its weight in gold. Taking an emphasis on cognitive and motor skill development, Wheels on the Bus has interactive illustrations and music available on several different instruments. If you're looking to improve your children's language and speaking from a preschool age, you'll appreciate Wheels on the Bus: they can learn the song in Spanish, French, German and Italian in addition to English.

If you or your child is one of those people that find hearing this tune akin to fingernails-on-a-chalkboard, you can shut off "Wheels on the Bus" at any time. You can still keep the sound effects on, however, meaning all the great gameplay remains.

quick review
★★★☆☆

Voice Toddler Cards

Developer: Sai Services + **Genre:** Education
Price: $0.99 + **Release:** May 31, 2009

Summary

A collection of talking flashcards for your toddler, Voice Toddler Cards is a great way to teach your child new words and new things. With over 200 different flashcards organized in nine different categories, your children will have an easy time moving their way through the cards as they need only swipe the screen to move on to the next. Created with real pictures and human voices, there's nothing artificial or mechanical about Voice Toddler Cards. Perfect for the home, road, plane or store, it's fun for your child, and educational too!

Why we like it

If you're a parent looking to raise a bilingual child, then buying Voice Toddler Cards in the App Store is a great option. The entire set is available in both English and Spanish from the get-go, making it a great bilingual learning tool. Even better, your child can get used to the sound of your voice if you decide to take advantage of another option: recording your own sounds for each card. Voice Toddler Cards are fun and feature big, captivating images, which will also help to keep that toddlin' toddler occupied.

[Not sure if you want to record your own voice for a card? Look in the corner of the screen: if there's a green dot, you've already made a recording. Want to revert back to the standard English or Spanish voices? It's easy to delete your recorded sounds too.]

Cute Math

Developer: Bokan Techologies **+ Genre:** Education
Price: $1.99 **+ Release:** June 14, 2009

> Summary

Looking for a fun and easy way to teach your children basic math skills? They'll have loads of fun counting penguins, placing apples into a basket, moving birds around for simple addition problems and dropping apples off trees for simple subtraction. Fantastic for preschool aged kids, Cute Math is a great way for kids to get a head start on other children before they set foot in kindergarten. It's never too early to get your child started with math, and Cute Math is a simple and fun App that lives up to its name because it's so darn cute!

> Why we like it

The interface is beautifully done. The graphics are top-notch, and every item is moveable—just drag and drop to solve simple math problems. For simple addition problems with two sets of items, one tap on the screen will move them all together, showing the principle of bringing two sets together and allowing your child to count up the items in total. Cute Math is one of the best basic math Apps in the App Store, and it will help provide the foundation your child needs to be successful in the early stages of math education.

Learn Chess

Developer: Tom Kerrigan ✦ **Genre:** Education
Price: FREE ✦ **Release:** February 18, 2009

Summary

Not every Education App is a paid App for younger children. Adults have a wide array of new things to learn too, and Learn Chess is a fantastic interactive e-book. Learn Chess teaches aspiring players of all ages everything they need to know to start down a path to becoming a Grand Master. Learn Chess takes advantage of your device's capabilities by using the touch screen to make for an interactive experience and allows you to demonstrate your knowledge by making moves on the chess board, not just playing them out in your head.

Why we like it

Learn Chess is short and simple, but it packs a ton of knowledge into its 118 pages. There are over 90 diagrams and nearly all of them are interactive, meaning you're able to perform what you've just learned before advancing. Learning all the terminology and some of the basic strategy is incredibly helpful as well—you'll be able to sit down and play with a friend as soon as you're done with the e-book portion.

Put your skills to the test with one of the other chess Apps from the same designer: Chess Lite and Pro. Follow your own progress and see if you can eventually master all three of Tom Kerrigan's kingly Apps.

Five Little Monkeys

Developer: LoeschWare ✦ **Genre:** Education
Price: $.099 ✦ **Release:** April 30, 2009

MAMA CALLED THE DOCTOR AND THE DOCTOR SAID

ONE FELL OFF AND BUMPED HIS HEAD

> Summary

Designed by the parents of toddlers, Five Little Monkeys is a simple educational App that is fun, bright and musical but also teaches your toddler counting skills. As the monkeys jump on the bed, your toddler builds counting as well as color recognition skills by adding and subtracting monkeys from the screen—just drag and drop the leaping friends or shake the device to clear them off. Featuring interactive objects such as an alarm clock and a monkey family portrait that your child can play with, this App has plenty of things to keep kids occupied.

> Why we like it

Kids of all ages love monkeys, and your toddler will cherish the creative freedom in Five Little Monkeys. If they see it on the screen, they can probably move it or interact with it in some way. The music isn't too bad either: there's a choice of a country, pop, or rock music for singing along. The words bounce across the bottom of the screen, and older toddlers may even learn how to read by singing along in karaoke fashion.

[
Want to put the jumpy monkeys back on the bed? Have your child tap on the number in the corner of the screen to watch them zoom back into the action. They'll have a blast adding monkeys to the screen and then shaking them back off.
]

quick review
★★★☆☆

Graphing Calculator

Developer: Gabor Nagy + **Genre:** Education
Price: $0.99 + **Release:** September 6, 2008

Summary

Need powerful but easy-to-use scientific calculations? Do you have to plot equations and points on a graph? Anytime you're looking for more functionality than a regular calculator, it's time to turn to Graphing Calculator. Need to remember a graph or function you just created? Take a screen shot and e-mail it to yourself or colleagues. Graphing Calculator features just about every common function you'll need for higher level mathematics and sciences in a powerful and easy-to-use package.

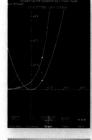

Why we like it

We've all been stuck without our calculators at one point or another, just when we needed them most. Never get stuck again thanks to the Graphing Calculator. There may be a learning curve (no pun intended) for the new user who uses only one type of graphing calculator, but in a pinch you'll be happy to have this App at your disposal for a buck.

[Graphing Calculator is a great App to have "just in case" if you're a student or professional that relies on having a calculator on hand at all times. You may find out very quickly, however, that Graphing Calculator can ably replace your old handheld graphing device.]

GRE Review

Developer: Watermelon Express + **Genre:** Education
Price: $0.99 + **Release:** May 6, 2009

> Summary

Need an extra lift when studying for your GRE? Looking to take something in the palm of your hand that you can read through on a car ride or on the train? It's worth your dollar to check out GRE Review. With several categories to prepare you for the test, including every Math, Verbal, and Writing component, GRE Review packs a ton of data into a nifty App. Every section of the App includes theory review, practice questions and tips and tricks that are easy to remember and that you can apply on the actual test.

> Why we like it

With a major test like the GRE, it never hurts to be as prepared as possible. When combined with other study guides and methods, GRE Review can be an incredibly useful supplemental App. The simple interface features over 500 pages of study material, meaning there's plenty to inform. Because of its intuitive interface and meaty content, anyone studying for this important test would benefit from spending the dollar to pick up GRE Review.

[Like GRE Review and want to take it one step further? Check out GRE Connect from Watermelon Express. It includes over 1,000 practice questions, diagnostic testing, and progress tracking tools to make sure you're on pace to be ready for the big day.]

quick review
★★★☆☆

Driver's Ed: Lite and Free

Developer: Eknath Kadam ✦ **Genre:** Education
Price: FREE ✦ **Release:** June 6, 2009

Summary

Preparing to take the written portion of your driving test or know someone who could use a little extra help? Driver's Ed covers everything you need to know before you take your driving test, from Rules of the Road to attitude and smart driving strategy. You can study by topic, taking in all the information on any of the subjects, including Hazard Awareness and Accidents. The App will randomly assign you questions with the p ractice test option, quizzing you on any or all of the categories. Zoom in and out to see graphics, get interactive explanations of complex maneuvers, and be as ready as you can be for your test!

Why we like it

The practice test feature is a great way to get ready for the test even while waiting in the perpetual lines at the DMV. It's quick and covers the mistakes you make immediately with explanations, ensuring that the concept sticks with you. You can review your progress from previous practice tests through bar charts and statistics to see where your weak areas are or identify your strengths. Having the driving handbooks from all 50 states is appreciated, since every state has its own quirks and laws.

[The App has detailed test results, making sure you get more out of Driver's Ed than just knowing what you got wrong. Knowing why you were wrong is just as important, and the positive reinforcement from learning the correct answer will help you get it right.]

Apps Capsules

❯ USA Factbook Free

Developer: ADS Software Group, Inc.
Genre: Education ✦ **Price:** FREE
Release: February 23, 2009

Featuring facts about all 50 states, USA Factbook Free is a great resource for learning a little more about the United States. It also features maps of the topography and highways of the country, and much more.

❯ The Chemical Touch: Lite Edition

Developer: Christopher Fennell ✦ **Genre:** Education
Price: FREE ✦ **Release:** December 13, 2009

When all you need is a simple periodic table of the elements, look no further than The Chemical Touch: Lite Edition. Featuring a display of the classic table, it provides more information about each element with just one tap.

❯ Toddler Match

Developer: Jason Booth ✦ **Genre:** Education
Price: $0.99 ✦ **Release:** June 16, 2009

With no menus to trigger, Toddler Match is a child-safe matching game for young ones aged one to four. Designed to help them make simple associations from picture selections, Toddler Match can be a handy occupation tool in a pinch.

❯ Preschool Adventure

Developer: 3DAL, LLC ✦ **Genre:** Education
Price: $0.99 ✦ **Release:** July 15, 2008

Containing six easy activities for parents to do with their toddlers, Preschool Adventure helps your child learn about counting and numbers. Kids will love it, especially the cute animals!

Art

Developer: ADS Software Group, Inc.
Genre: Education ✦ **Price:** $0.99
Release: February 10, 2009

Featuring some of the world's greatest artists and their masterpieces, Art is a great way to learn about over 400 different works from the masters to the modern. The App includes information about each painting and a quiz game.

Daily Spotlight

Developer: Ethan Productions ✦ **Genre:** Education
Price: FREE ✦ **Release:** June 15, 2009

Daily Spotlight lets you learn about someone new, someone either currently famous or historical, every day. Open it daily for a biography about someone who has helped to shape our world.

Math Drills Lite

Developer: Instant Interactive ✦ **Genre:** Education
Price: FREE ✦ **Release:** January 21, 2009

A simple but attractive math environment, Math Drills Lite helps a student learn addition, subtraction, multiplication and division. Featuring tips and tricks for figuring out the solutions, Math Drills Lite can help any young student.

Suzy Dress Up

Developer: 3DAL, LLC ✦ **Genre:** Education
Price: $0.99 ✦ **Release:** January 15, 2009

Customize the outfits of Suzy Dress Up and learn creative thinking at the same time. Your girl will love choosing from the hundreds of different options and letting her imagination run wild.

TV.com

Developer: CBS Interactive **+ Genre:** Entertainment
Price: FREE **+ Release:** February 25, 2009

▸ Summary

Personalized TV that works whether you're in WiFi or a 3G coverage area, TV.com is an App that's almost too good to be true. With a vast list of featured shows and videos, including full episodes of CBS shows, there's something in TV.com for everyone. You can make playlists, add favorites to come back to at any time, and search from anywhere within the App for live search results. Easy navigation and tons of video content make this an almost must-have App!

▸ Why we like it

It's hard to believe this App is free! Beyond all the information packed into the TV.com App, there's so much video content that it's astounding to imagine it doesn't cost a dime. More full-length episodes are being added all the time and you can use keywords to create your own custom "feed" of videos. There are loads of extra content too—beyond the regular TV shows and updates, you can also view reviews from CNET.com's experts about the world of consumer electronics.

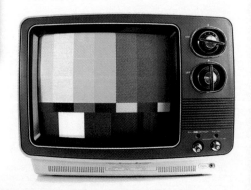

quick review
★★★☆☆

6500+ Cool Facts

Developer: Webwork and Applications
Genre: Entertainment **+ Price:** FREE
Release: May 11, 2009

Summary

The name of the App says it all—an App packed with fun and interesting facts about all sorts of wild, crazy, and even mundane topics. Easy-to-use controls mean you can just swipe in any direction to uncover a different fact. 6500+ Cool Facts is a free App with tons of cool information. For example, a group of geese is called a "gaggle" on the ground and a "skein" in the air. Learn tons more from 6500+ Cool Facts.

Whe... ...he blue b... ...is the loudest ...ound produced by any animal

Why we like it

If you're stuck waiting in the airport or standing in a long line, 6500+ Cool Facts may help you save your sanity. This App works well because it focuses on one thing and does it well. The App is constantly evolving with new updates and facts, so be on the lookout for new versions as they come out. In the meantime, make time slip by just a little bit faster with 6500+ Cool Facts.

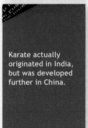

Karate actually originated in India, but was developed further in China.

A single cup of gasoline, when ignited, has the same explosive power as five sticks of dynamite.

Like 6500+ Cool Facts but think you've exhausted the entire list? By the time you work your way through the entire App, a new version will probably be on its way to the App Store, and it'll still be free.

quick review
★★★☆☆

Family Guy

Developer: Fox Mobile Entertainment, Inc.
Genre: Entertainment
Price: $1.99 + **Release:** June 16, 2009

❯ Summary

The animated hit Family Guy has made it to the App Store with a debut that's, as Peter would say, "freakin' sweet." Enjoy the outstanding clips featuring some of the biggest laughs from all seven seasons of the show. Play fun Family Guy mini games that will have you laughing along with your favorite characters. Plus, Family Guy never gets stale—the App is updated daily with new clips that will make you go "giggity!"

❯ Why we like it

Unlike the Apps for some other TV shows, Family Guy gives you extras that you might expect from Seth MacFarlane and company. You can toss an animated Peter around the screen, moving him through multiple backgrounds. Swapping heads and bodies on Stewie also makes for some laughs. The App does not have full episodes, which is a bit of a downside, but the information for each clip tells you what episode it came from and provides a direct link to buy the full show from the iTunes Store.

> Use the sharing features when you're together with friends to share your favorite mixes of clips, giving them titles based on your favorite Family Guy quotes. Be on the lookout for hidden content in the App, since you never know what might pop up!

quick review
★★★☆☆

AT&T Mobile Remote Access

Developer: AT&T, Inc ✛ **Genre:** Entertainment
Price: FREE ✛ **Release:** June 12, 2009

Summary

An App from the people that bring you iPhone access, AT&T Mobile Remote Access is just as much a must-have as your cell signal if you're a subscriber to AT&T's U-Verse television service. More than just a guide to what's on TV, AT&T Mobile Remote Access gives you full control over your Total Home DVR. Think you're at a baseball game where there might be a no-hitter? Set your home DVR from your seat to make sure you capture the final innings. Watching a movie with a friend? Set it to record at home so you can watch the rest later.

Why we like it

This is so fast, easy-to-use and reliable, you'll wonder how you watched television before you started programming your DVR remotely. With two weeks of listings packed in at one time, there's no chance you'll miss your favorites when you get back home. The search option is also well done, allowing you to wade through the listings to find exactly what you're looking for, even including programs starring your favorite actors from other shows! Additionally, AT&T Mobile Remote Access is truly an all-mobile App as it doesn't need WiFi or even a 3G connection to work properly.

[Just looking to record your favorite shows in HD? You can filter your search results to show such things as HD only, find only new episodes of your shows or just ones you haven't seen before and even bookmark channels to easily find your favorites.]

quick review

★★★☆☆

Babelgum

Developer: Babelgum + **Genre:** Entertainment
Price: FREE + **Release:** March 11, 2009

❯ Summary

Your gateway to thousands of hours of music, laughter, drama and even horror, Babelgum lets you explore hundreds of different media outlets. You can rock out with some of your favorite bands, laugh along with the Onion and Onion News Network, get serious with the BBC or even learn a bit more about Earth with a nature program. Featuring lots of free content and easy access to paid content, Babelgum is useful for anyone looking to either find something new or for old favorites.

❯ Why we like it

There are plenty of ways to search for your favorite videos with Babelgum: beyond a basic search, there are options to find hand-picked Highlights, check out the Most Viewed clips from other users, and even your bookmarked Favorites. Sharing is a snap as Babelgum allows you to pass along favorite clips to friends via e-mail or through Facebook and MySpace. Providing you with fast access to your favorite clips, Babelgum has a lot to like, and being able to buy the full version of just about every clip is a welcome convenience.

[Tired of looking at the standard stack view or want to make finding your favorite Highlights a bit easier? Double-tap any black portion of your screen and a handy list view lets you sort through the clips the old-fashioned way. Shake your device to refresh Highlights.]

quick review
★★★★☆

Cooliris

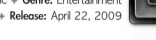

Developer: Cooliris, Inc ◆ **Genre:** Entertainment
Price: FREE ◆ **Release:** April 22, 2009

Summary

Want to follow breaking news stories, track your favorite videos and share all of the content with your family and friends? Look no further than the slick interface of Cooliris. The 3D wall you're presented with is fully customizable, bringing you the content you want to see. With news from around the world you can always stay apprised of the latest action while you comment on a photo in your Flickr account or Tweet about the video you just watched. Everything features full metadata, letting you know exactly when and where the content is from.

Why we like it

It's a 3D wall that's always streaming, which is worth the download just to see in action. Cooliris is just flat out cool—there's nothing like it in the App Store or anywhere else. Zoom in on your favorites, tap once for full-screen and even e-mail anything you like. There are so many ways to access and share what you see, you'll have to try each way at least once. There are many options for saving, including direct downloading to your device, a web service to keep track of your favorites, and built-in bookmarking.

[Cooliris features full integration with Twitter. If you use the service, you can Tweet directly from any video or news story, putting a fresh spin on story commentary. The App also fully integrates with Flickr, enabling both sharing and commenting.]

Fluid 2

Developer: Fabien Sanglard + **Genre:** Entertainment
Price: $0.99 + **Release:** June 10, 2009

> Summary

Need to relax for a few minutes? Check out the soothing interactive waters of Fluid 2. Looking to keep the kids occupied for a bit? They too can find fun in Fluid 2: moving fingers across the screen and watching the water react is just like the real thing, only without getting wet! Watch bubbles and patterns emerge and disappear, and see how the water is affected by the speed you put behind your motions. With a full set of options to customize your water, you'll be relaxed in no time.

> Why we like it

The original App is popular, with over 1.5 million downloads, and Fluid 2 is much improved. The first App was relaxing to be sure, but the cool new features of Fluid 2 really set it apart. You can turn on the optional music track to make the mood even more relaxed, change the color and viscosity of the water and use any background you want, including any photos you've taken. Simple, soothing and relaxing, Fluid 2 helps to ease the mind and get away for a few minutes.

[Think that the background of Fluid 2 looks like it could be part of a fountain? Make a wish and toss a coin, a new option in the App. You can throw as many coins as you want into the water, watching them sink down just like the real thing.]

quick review
★★★☆☆

OrbLive

Developer: Orb Networks ✦ **Genre:** Entertainment
Price: $9.99 ✦ **Release:** February 9, 2009

Summary

Wish you could watch live TV, access all of your music and videos from home or keep track of your webcams but not sure how to do it when out and about? Check out OrbLive, a media center solution that brings astounding functionality to your iPhone and iPod Touch. You never have to worry about syncing your media or picking and choosing what goes onto your device when you have too much: OrbLive will sort it all for you and give you access to everything, on demand. There's also no need to convert files to play on your device since OrbLive handles encoding for you.

Why we like it

Orb is an easy solution for people who aren't sure about setting up a home media server. There's very little work involved, and just about anyone can do it. The Orb platform is versatile—you can use it on home TVs over a network, access it on any computer you happen come across, or even run the application on video game systems.

[Want to see just how powerful Orb is but not sure if you're ready to take the plunge yet? Check out the free version of OrbLive. The free version takes three pieces of media from every category in your library, letting you check out all the features of the full App.]

iDoodle2 lite

Developer: Josiah Larson **+ Genre:** Entertainment
Price: FREE **+ Release:** March 27, 2009

Summary

Though the word 'lite' may make it seem like there's not much fun to be had with iDoodle2 lite, think again. It's a full-featured App with user friendly functions like savable settings, a multi-step Undo and an easy-to-use Kid mode for the young ones. There's plenty here to awaken your inner Leonardo. With multiple brushes, lines and filling options for the impressive color palette, the options are virtually endless. An adjustable offset even allows for precision control—you can move the pointer away from your finger to better see what you're working on.

Why we like it

In its free form, iDoodle2 lite is one of the best drawing Apps in the App Store. One feature that other doodling Apps fall short on is the Zoom feature. iDoodle2 lite has a pinpoint-accurate Zoom that really lets you get in close for detailed work. If you find iDoodle2 lite is exactly what you're looking for, check out the full version that has even more brushes and options to help you paint your masterpiece!

[Need inspiration? Look around online and in the App Store for some of the best creations with iDoodle and iDoodle2. There are some amazing pieces of art that people have posted, both mimicking real classics and creating their own original works.]

quick review
★★★★☆

TRANSFORMERS CyberToy

Developer: Glu ✦ **Genre:** Entertainment
Price: $0.99 ✦ **Release:** June 17, 2009

Summary

Are you a fan of the blockbuster movie series, the classic cartoon, or both? The TRANSFORMERS CyberToy is more than meets the eye, featuring Bumblebee from the new Revenge of the Fallen movie. Action Figure mode allows you to pose Bumblebee and check out his stats and character history, and CyberToy has everything you remember about the great action figures of the past. Puzzle Mode will put your brain to the test, making you think quickly to reassemble or disassemble Bumblebee. Click, tap, drag and tilt your way to making him a car or a full-featured Transformer.

Why we like it

It's a digital action figure unlike anything else out there. With the power of Transformers, the App is perfect for keeping your kids occupied with one of their favorite machines or for first generation fans reliving their childhood. Action Mode brings you everything fun about having an action figure without worrying about losing small parts or breaking the toy, while Puzzle Mode is a fun twist on seeing who can solve the puzzle fastest—great for playing with friends. A masterpiece!

[Want to stay in touch with the makers of the CyberToy to check for updates coming to the App? You can follow the Twitter feed of the developers or become a fan on Facebook and be the first to know when Megatron and Optimus Prime crash the App Store!]

quick review
★★★☆☆

PhoneFlicks

Developer: Next Mobile Web + **Genre:** Entertainment
Price: FREE + **Release:** September 15, 2008

Summary

New releases, old classics and your favorite TV shows are waiting for you with Phone-Flicks! The perfect App for the millions of Netflix subscribers, PhoneFlicks uses a sleek interface to put all the power of Netflix in the palm of your hand. You can view all of your recent activity, read your recommendations and reviews, and even add or delete movies in your queue with just a few taps.

Why we like it

With over 100,000 movies in its catalog, Netflix has become the biggest name in movie rentals because their the service is easy, reliable and inexpensive. PhoneFlicks is an extension of this usability—being able to access your queue and favorites and browse through the catalog away from home is incredibly handy. If you have a Netflix account, PhoneFlicks will quickly become an essential addition to your Apps library. You might never visit the web interface again.

quick review
★★★☆☆

Type Drawing

Developer: Hansol Huh ✦ **Genre:** Entertainment
Price: $0.99 ✦ **Release:** June 4, 2009

Summary

Type Drawing is simple, but has a big twist—it's a drawing App that uses letters. You can use sentences, words, or even individual letters to get started, and the drawing comes very naturally. With many colors and backgrounds to choose from, every drawing is unique. A community supported App that will leave you laughing at what you can come up with, Type Drawing lets you save your favorites to your photo album, share them with friends, or even make your newest creation a background.

Why we like it

There are plenty of options to give this App depth and variety. Setting the font, colors, size and opacity of the drawing lets you tweak your creations to be as unique as you are. The latest version packs in even more features, the most handy of which is the Undo and Redo option, giving you leeway to go back or forward 20 steps. Text Size Control gives you even more customization options, and the new fonts make drawings more interesting than ever.

Type Drawing is not just limited to the iPhone and iPod Touch; it's a concept that's been almost five years in the making. The project has been live since 2005 and many different artists have contributed. Check out the Flickr account of the developers to see what others are doing.

quick review
★★★☆☆

VLC Remote

Developer: Hobbyist Software ✦ **Genre:** Entertainment
Price: $2.99 ✦ **Release:** April 27, 2009

▸ Summary

Looking for a way to control your media library in your favorite player from across the room? Never go reaching for the mouse to adjust your media again thanks to VLC Remote, a fantastic companion to the VLC media player. VLC Remote offers you full browsing control—you can play any media on your home machine with ease. Browsing and searching is a snap, and the controls make it simple to adjust for full-screen, volume, and playback. You can even search external hard drives and queue up playlists.

▸ Why we like it

The desktop VLC player is a terrific media player. It's lightweight, easy to download and use, and best of all, it can play just about anything. It's a versatile program, handling just about anything you throw at it, and the App follows suit. If you're a user of the desktop App, available on any major operating system, adding VLC Remote should almost be required. Browsing, playing, and controlling your files is an absolute snap, and being able to tap into your media from across the room is always handy.

> Not sure if VLC Remote is worth trying out? Download the desktop software and see for yourself. It works on every major operating system, from Windows to Mac to just about every flavor of Linux.

quick review
★★★★☆

What's On TV?

Developer: NapkinStudio.com + **Genre:** Entertainment
Price: FREE + **Release:** August 23, 2008

Summary ⓒ

On the go and wondering when your favorite show is on? Are you curious if your regional network is available where you're at? The free App What's On TV is a fast and elegant solution for looking up the TV listings wherever you are, no matter who the provider is. Search your home listings, browse the HD lineup or look for favorite shows, and more. If you're looking to share info with a friend, What's On TV lets you quickly e-mail listings with a few taps.

Why we like it ⓒ

If you don't want to tie yourself to the specific listings for your provider or they don't offer an App, then What's On TV is a must-have. You can look up the listings anywhere, from your house to a vacation hotel room to grandma's house. If you're looking to see the listings where you are but you're not sure what the ZIP code is, What's On TV can use iPhone GPS to figure out where you are and what providers service the area. With over 11,000 channels and 13,000 providers in the United States and Canada, those oldschool days of channel surfing are gone for good!

Watch TV in many different places and want to keep your channels organized? What's On TV allows you to save multiple favorites so you can get quick access to the listings wherever you are.

Apps Capsules

❯ Alternate Endings

Developer: Jonathan Huer
Genre: Entertainment ✦ **Price:** $0.99
Release: November 18, 2008

Control overwhelmed security guard Russell Bingham in this live-action, choose-your-own-adventure movie! Your choices will make the difference—tap the screen to make a choice or shake for a random decision.

❯ Lightsaber Unleashed

Developer: The Mac Box ✦ **Genre:** Entertainment
Price: FREE ✦ **Release:** September 24, 2008

One of the most popular Apps in its category, Lightsaber Unleashed is a must-have for any fan of Star Wars. Wave your lightsaber around with real sound effects and choose your character of choice from Force Unleashed.

❯ Remote

Developer: Apple, Inc. ✦ **Genre:** Entertainment
Price: FREE ✦ **Release:** April 2, 2009

An incredibly nifty App for the technologically savvy iPhone or iPod Touch user, Remote lets you control the music or video on your computer or Apple TV with your device.

❯ DIRECTV

Developer: DIRECTV, Inc. ✦ **Genre:** Entertainment
Price: FREE ✦ **Release:** March 30, 2009

Stuck away from home and want to set up a recording on your home DVR? No problem if you have DIRECTV. Browse through the listings of shows and movies and record to any DVR in your house.

Joost

Developer: Joost, Inc. + **Genre:** Entertainment
Price: FREE + **Release:** November 17, 2008

Browse through tens of thousands of video clips
from your favorite movies and TV shows with
Joost. Thousands of hours of content are available
in all genres, from anime to documentaries.

TMZ

Developer: Telepictures Productions
Genre: Entertainment + **Price:** FREE
Release: January 15, 2009

Stay on top of the latest entertainment news and
gossip with the leading internet authority, TMZ. With
exclusive stories and high quality videos from TMZ
TV, it's a must-have for entertainment fanatics.

Bubblewrap

Developer: Orsome + **Genre:** Entertainment
Price: FREE + **Release:** July 6, 2008

Accept no substitutes! Sometimes you just need to
pop a few bubbles and blow off some steam: turn
to Bubblewrap. Pop as many as you can within the
time limit.

Artisan

Developer: Elements of Design + **Genre:** Entertainment
Price: $0.99 + **Release:** February 6, 2009

A creative way to relax your mind or ignite
creativity, Artisan puts art at your finger tips.
Control the flow of the brushes with your fingers or
let Artisan randomly initiate.

Bloomberg

Developer: Bloomberg LP + **Genre:** Finance
Price: FREE + **Release:** May 30, 2008

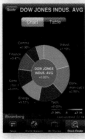

> Summary

Investing has truly gone global, and staying a half-step ahead of other investors is a major challenge in the 24/7 world we now live in. When you're on the go, trust Bloomberg for the financial news, notes, and advice that you need to stay ahead in the game. Create a customized list of your investments and allow the Bloomberg App to track them for you and deliver exclusive information about the company and its stock's performance.

> Why we like it

Bloomberg is one of the world's most trusted sources for news about the financial world, and it's all available in real-time on your device. With quotes on just about any type of securities trading, Bloomberg gives you the tools to help you make smarter trades. News and analysis are constantly updated through-out the day, and the charts are exceptional—easy to read on the small screen and tightly packed with rich data.

quick review
★★★☆☆

Checkbook

Developer: Jeremy Jacob ✦ **Genre:** Finance
Price: FREE ✦ **Release:** February 21, 2009

Summary ◐

Tired of lugging around an oldschool checkbook when you don't even write checks anymore but still want to keep track of your checking account? There's no more popular solution than using Checkbook. Quick and convenient, Checkbook allows you to record transactions, save monthly recurring events like bills and even schedule other transactions you know are coming in the near future. It's also great if you have multiple checkbooks to track: Checkbook lets you organize your accounts and total spending as a group or individually with the information sorted however you wish.

Why we like it ◐

Balancing a checkbook has somehow become a lost art in the digital age. With account tracking on credit cards and other forms of payment updating instantaneously, it is a hassle to have to whip out a pen and balance a checkbook to keep all your finances straight and current. Checkbook changes all that with speed and convenience. All your information can be password protected, and you'll never have to spend time in the register again.

[Checkbook will automatically keep track of your information across different checkbooks and the data updates immediately. You can view the information with or without scheduled expenses, allowing you to see the information the way you want.]

iXpenseIt

Developer: FYI Mobileware, Inc **+ Genre:** Finance
Price: $4.99 **+ Release:** May 19, 2009

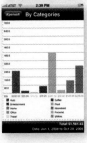

> ## Summary

Want to know what you're spending, where your money is going, and see it all crisply and clearly? Check out iXpenseIt, a useful tracking tool that lets you record any purchase within seconds. Want to remember the information from a receipt but feel you may lose it? Snap a picture and let iXpenseIt store the image for you. It's so much better than using bulky software on your home computer to do the same function as you always have your phone with you. And since it only takes seconds to use, you can have your expenses accounted for before you even leave the register.

> ## Why we like it

This App is featured in television ads for the iPhone, and it's easy to see why. It's the simplest way to aggregate expenses on the device, period. It's an innovative, elegant and powerful tool designed to be used by anyone. With a battery meter representing how much of your monthly budget remains, it's easy to keep track of your finances at a glance. The App features logical categories, and setting up monthly expenses like rent and electricity as automatic expenses only takes a few taps.

[iXpenseIt is fantastic for the home user, but it's plenty flexible and powerful enough for a businessperson on the road. In addition to tracking all expenses, it even has a mileage tracker that lets you know how much ground you've covered.]

quick review
★★★★☆

Mint.com

Developer: Mint.com + **Genre:** Finance
Price: FREE + **Release:** December 15, 2008

Summary ◄

If you want to keep track of all of your
accounts at any time without having to use
multiple Apps, Mint is a refreshing option. An
impressive and free tracker for all of your
spending and monetary functions, Mint.com
has brought its critically acclaimed tracking
service to the iPhone and iPod Touch.
Seamlessly bringing together information from
even rival financial institutions, Mint will wow
you with its speed and capabilities. And by
bringing everything together in one cohesive
interface, Mint can help you get a clearer
picture of your financial life.

Why we like it ◄

Mint's categories really help users track
exactly where their money goes. The
information is easily accessible and lets you
see how much money is going to living
expenses, how much you're spending on
food and entertainment, and even how much
money is left in each budget for the month.
You can even get a breakdown of how much
money you've been spending in the iTunes
Store on Apps! It's also nice to be able to
view information about investments, including
the performance of a 401(k) and IRA.

> Concerned about identity theft or losing your data? As long as you
> know your Mint.com account info, you can see if there have been any
> unusual expenses across all your accounts. If they detect anything
> suspicious, Mint will let you know—possibly even before your bank.

quick review
★★★☆☆

Mortgage Calculator

Developer: Raizlabs Corporation + **Genre:** Finance
Price: $0.99 + **Release:** April 19, 2009

❯ Summary

Perfect for house hunters and real estate professionals, Mortgage Calculator combines a simple interface with the powerful functionality of making financial calculations on the fly. Starting with property cost and allowing you to punch in variables from there, Mortgage Calculator has enough features to give you detailed information yet is easy enough for anyone to use. Capable of handling one-time costs, monthly and yearly expenses like taxes, and creating an amortization schedule, Mortgage Calculator can do it all in the world of home finances.

❯ Why we like it

Mortgage Calculator adjusts for the real world. The App seamlessly handles the variables that come with any home loan. For example, if there's a homeowner's association fee to pay, insurance to be bought or taxes to be added, Mortgage Calculator can accommodate. The App handles variable year options and conveniently allows you to calculate price per square foot. With large buttons and an easy-to-use interface, Mortgage Calculator won't overwhelm you, but it will tell you the vital facts that you need to know. And if you're just punching in various scenarios, remember to just shake to clear your screen!

[Like the idea behind Mortgage Calculator but not sure what else you can use it for? Don't limit yourself to just the function of the App's title. You can calculate a personal loan, home equity, or even a car loan using this handy App.]

quick review
★★★☆☆

PortfolioLive

Developer: Turing Studios **+ Genre:** Finance
Price: $5.99 **+ Release:** April 28, 2009

Summary

Wondering how your portfolio is performing at any time? Featuring real time, up-to-the-minute stock prices from the New York Stock Exchange and NASDAQ along with delayed results for other U.S. markets, PortfolioLive can calculate your instant gains and losses across multiple portfolios. It doesn't matter who your broker is, or even if you have multiple brokerage accounts—you can organize it all in PortfolioLive. You can even calculate your commission fees right along with your stocks.

Why we like it

This is what business on the iPhone and iPod Touch is all about. With a full list of your positions and easy-to-read fonts, you can get the core data you want right away. Every category can be sorted, which makes your portfolios fully customizable. A nifty pop-up on the bottom of the screen shows your current net gain/loss, so you can see the big picture as well. It's not all just about stocks either—PortfolioLive lets you view data on commodities, options, futures and even foreign exchanges.

Worried about how the updates of PortfolioLive will affect your battery life? The settings options let you change how frequently your information refreshes, so if you don't need to know real-time info as quickly, you can make the App reload less frequently.

Apps Capsules

▣ ATM Hunter

Developer: MasterCard ✦ **Genre:** Finance
Price: FREE ✦ **Release:** March 24, 2009

MasterCard's ATM Hunter will help you find an
ATM wherever you are. If you want to use your
own bank or do other banking functions, the search
function allows you to narrow down your options.

▣ Amortize

Developer: Interlook Corp. ✦ **Genre:** Finance
Price: FREE ✦ **Release:** August 30, 2008

Would you like to know just how much you'll be
paying per month or just want to view your amortization schedule? Look no further than this simple
App, which does all the calculations for you.

▣ Bankarama

Developer: General UI, LLC ✦ **Genre:** Finance
Price: $5.99 ✦ **Release:** May 5, 2009

Keep track of your spending with Bankarama.
Record your transactions as soon as you make
them and be confident in knowing what your
account balance is. All information is secured
with a password.

▣ Bank of Me

Developer: Architechies ✦ **Genre:** Finance
Price: $0.99 ✦ **Release:** April 6, 2009

Having trouble remembering your IOUs? Record
your debts to others (and theirs to you) with Bank
of Me. Adding a name is as simple as three taps
and the App can even send e-mail reminders.

Blackgold

Developer: Toughturtle + **Genre:** Finance
Price: FREE + **Release:** May 17, 2009

With the massive fluctuations in the cost of oil,
gasoline, gold, and natural gas in the last few years,
following the prices has never been more
important. Keep track of these natural resources as
their values rise and fall.

CBS MoneyWatch

Developer: CBS Interactive + **Genre:** Finance
Price: FREE + **Release:** April 20, 2009

Keep track of the daily market activity on the go with
CBS MoneyWatch. With a clean interface and fast
streaming video, CBS MoneyWatch is a great destination for respected financial analysis and advice.

Cha-Ching

Developer: Midnight Apps, Inc. + **Genre:** Finance
Price: $2.99 + **Release:** March 21, 2009

Manage and control your budget and monitor your
spending habits with Cha-Ching. It integrates with
your life on the go, and can sync your transaction
history from the desktop Cha-Ching software.

Cheapest

Developer: Formula Sensei + **Genre:** Finance
Price: $0.99 + **Release:** December 20, 2008

Faced with two different size options at the store
and not sure which one is the better deal? Enter the
data of both items and Cheapest figures out which
one is a better value.

ABM Command

Developer: Side Project Games, LLC + **Genre:** Games
Price: $0.99 + **Release:** May 7, 2009

▶ Summary

ABM Command, formerly titled DEFCON 1, is possibly the best missile defense game available in the App Store. Use antiballistic missiles (the ABM in the game's title) to defend your cities against a bombardment of enemy ICBMs. And once you clear the skies of MIRVs, turn the tables and fire your missiles right back at the enemy. Levels are broken up into days, and after each day you are presented with the option of purchasing both offensive and defensive weapons from your arms dealer, who can help you get the upper hand on your enemy.

▶ Why we like it

For a simple idea, this game has slick graphics and controls combined with surprising depth. Additionally, the graphics of the missiles in the air and exploding are positively boom-tiful. The arsenal of weapons available for purchase includes all sorts of missiles—from smart bombs to massive bunker busters, you can choose your weapons of mass destruction! Defensively, you can deploy anti-aircraft guns, defensive missiles, and even hold national parties to revive your cities. In total, there are six national factions and each has its strengths and weaknesses, so choose wisely.

[Your weapons and cities on the ground may not look like much, but wait until the fireworks start. The graphics look fantastic, rivaling the explosions of any game in the App Store. The ability to counter-attack is an especially satisfying twist.]

quick review
★★★★☆

a bug's defense

Developer: CDE **+ Genre:** Games
Price: $0.99 **+ Release:** June 17, 2009

Summary

This game is a relative newcomer to the App Store but is already buzzing with popularity because it's so much fun to play. Lucy's home has been invaded by bugs and it's your job to shoo and swat and get them out of her house. Keep the bugs away from Lucy—a green bar at the top of the screen indicates her tolerance for the bugs in her home. If that bar runs out, Lucy will faint, and that's not a good thing.

Why we like it

Though simple, a bug's defense is tough to conquer. There are three unique chapters to the game, each with three levels. It can be a challenge to manage your money in the game and you may even need to sell a weapon to raise cash, something you don't see often in games today. But selling weapons may diminish your arsenal in the garden, making it tougher to eliminate the waves and waves of bugs that will be descending upon you.

[
It's always important to remember that in a bug's defense, Lucy is afraid of the bugs! You have to keep them out of her house or else she won't want to go out to a movie or even step outside to be impressed with your bug-zapping abilities.
]

quick review
★★★★☆

Ace Commando

Developer: Meridian + **Genre:** Games
Price: $0.99 + **Release:** June 18, 2009

▶ Summary

With a deep story about Mars Federation commando Jack, who has come to Earth to infiltrate the mysterious HANDS organization, Ace Commando has stormed into the App Store with 12 levels of shooting goodness. With three different difficulties to choose from, Ace Commando is as difficult as you want it to be. Controlling Jack is a breeze, as the game allows you to blend your choice of touch or accelerometer controls.

▶ Why we like it

Meridian makes some top-notch games and this title is no exception. Having two different ways to control your commando is a welcome feature in this game, as it's always nice to have options when moving them around. The dynamic boss AI works well and makes the end of each level a challenge to complete. The graphics and music for this game are top notch, and the dynamic ranking system helps you to compare yourself against everyone else playing Ace Commando.

[If you're having trouble controlling your player, make sure to pause the game and recalibrate your device. Doing so can make the difference between navigating your commando through a level or getting jacked by the next enemy you face.]

quick review
★★★★☆

:Shift:

Developer: Armor Games, Inc. + **Genre:** Games
Price: $0.99 + **Release:** May 1, 2009

Summary

As subject 32763, you are a member of an experiment gone awry. The popularity of this game, already played by over 10 million people online, has carried over to its App version. A puzzle-based platform game with several twists, :Shift: pulses to the beat of its own original soundtrack. The original got rave reviews by the millions that played it, but many complained the game was too short: that's fixed in the pulsating App Store version. This game is hot.

Why we like it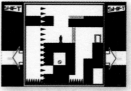

:Shift: has gotten rave reviews from just about everyone who tries it, and it's easy to see why. There's nothing else like it out there. The graphics look awesome, not because they're eye-popping, but because the game looks elegant and minimalist and sets the stage ideally for a unique experience. The controls make full use of your device's motion-sensing capabilities. The App Store version has 25 new levels that aren't in the original, meaning that even if you've played :Shift: before, there's something new for you too.

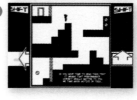

[Stuck without your iPhone or iPod Touch? You can play :Shift: on the web. It's the original version of the game designed before the App version was ever conceived. It's the same great action, but there just aren't as many levels and obviously the controls are different.]

quick review
★★★★☆

TOP GUN

Developer: Paramount Digital Entertainment
Genre: Games ✦ **Price:** $2.99 ✦ **Release:** May 5, 2009

Summary

As a hotshot recruit to the TOP GUN school under iconic movie characters Maverick and Ice Man, it's up to you to become the U.S. Navy's next top pilot. With a hostile threat taking to the skies over Navy airspace, you'll be flying on the front lines. Take control of your brand-new F-22 jet and hop in for some outstanding aerobatic combat! Shoot down enemy jets, dodge missiles, and navigate hostile environments on the "Highway to the Danger Zone"!

Why we like it

Like other games in the App Store, this one holds the interest of a certain group of people just for the nostalgia factor. A whole generation of kids grew up wishing they were Maverick or Ice Man, and this is the best looking TOP GUN game of all time. The 3D animation is silky smooth and the controls with the accelerometer are very responsive: just make sure to pause and recalibrate if you move around a lot. Having two planes to fly in more than 10 missions means this game has depth to go along with its surprising looks.

[Fans of the flick should watch and listen for shout-outs to the movie mixed in throughout the game. When your plane is in danger, for instance, the screen will flash "Danger Zone," a tribute to the famous Kenny Loggins song from the movie.]

quick review
★★★☆☆

Amateur Surgeon

Developer: adult swim + **Genre:** Games
Price: $2.99 + **Release:** December 4, 2008

Summary

Ever dream of becoming a doctor? Sure you have. But at the end of the day you're most likely unwashed, unqualified, and wholly unsuited to be a surgeon. That's the premise of Amateur Surgeon from the cartoon masters at (adult swim). They take the idea that you would have absolutely no idea in the emergency room and run with it. Operate on patients with a pizza cutter, salad tongs, staplers and car batteries and hack your way through 27 different surgeries. Each surgery is a complicated, multi-step procedure, and be sure to look out for the robot level!

Why we like it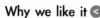

Games that feature great graphics can sometimes take themselves too seriously. Other games focus on the funny, but gameplay can seem an afterthought. Amateur Surgeon manages to combine gameplay and funny into one hilariously disgusting App. This balance really makes the App shine, and while the subject matter might make some queasy, this really is a solid game. The controls are witty as well—there's something oddly satisfying about rubbing the screen to spread gels and cauterize wounds.

Games

Aerial Combat

Developer: App Tech Studios + **Genre:** Games
Price: $0.99 + **Release:** June 18, 2009

⊳ Summary

As the enemy planes streak by, do you have the skill and timing to shoot them down? The brilliantly simple Aerial Combat puts your abilities to the test. Avoid enemy fire while moving in your boat, or even shoot boats out of the water in any of Aerial Combat's three game modes. With two levels of difficulty, this title is playable by all. With simple but attractive graphics and special extras like high score leader boards, this game is sure to never leave you over-bored.

⊳ Why we like it

Aerial Combat does a lot of little things right, which means the developers took the time to polish the game properly. You can't fire the guns over and over again—you have to wait for them to reload. Bullets aren't unlimited either as you have to conserve and wait for more or you run the risk of running out and losing the game. The game is not easy, but it is accessible to all and the simple "tap and tilt" controls and collision detection are outstanding.

[It may be best to think of Aerial Combat as three different games
instead of one game with three levels. Each one is unique and has its
own high score boards to shoot for. The game is still being updated,
so look for new and exciting features to come.]

quick review
★★★☆☆

Pig Air

Developer: Icarus Interactive, LLC + **Genre:** Games
Price: $1.99 + **Release:** June 18, 2009

Summary

Has anyone ever told you that something would happen "when pigs fly"? They'd better come up with something new now that pigs are going airborne in Pig Air. Use science and invention to attach wings and jets to pigs and jettison them through the air as far as possible, while also trying to keep them airborne the longest. Launch your pig from the top of his silo and see just how far he'll go! Earn cash with each flight to purchase extra gear to try and help your pig fly farther.

Why we like it

There's a lot to oink about in Pig Air. The controls are simple, the idea is fun, and the store brings an extra level of depth to the game. Built-in leader boards allow you to compare your best time and distance with players all around the world, and now you can even compete with the best of the best over the internet. Best of all, Pig Air knows it's supposed to be a silly game. It is always ready to provide you with a laugh just when you need it.

[
Not content with just trying for the high score on the leader boards? Stick with Pig Air because the developers say there is an update in the works that will add a Challenge Mode so you can compete with other Pig Air players around the world.
]

quick review
★★★★★

World Cup Ping Pong

Developer: Skyworks + **Genre:** Games
Price: $0.99 + **Release:** May 1, 2009

> Summary

Think that just because you have a ping pong table in your basement that you're an expert? Test your skills with World Cup Ping Pong, the premier table tennis game in the App Store. World Cup Ping Pong features four different modes: work on your skills in Practice Mode, challenge the computer in Arcade Mode, work your way through the brackets in Tournament Mode, or play a friend in Head-to-Head Mode. There's something in this title for every fan of ping pong, and it can be as simple as knocking the ball back-and-forth or as tough as putting wicked spins on the ball.

> Why we like it

After playing all the popular ping pong, table tennis, and beer pong games from the App Store, we decided this one is probably the standout of the bunch. It's an arcade game but with stunning physics: the spin is different with each paddle, and applying just the right amount of spin and angle is key to defeating opponents as you move through the levels. The graphics are also notable for being silky smooth.

[Don't like the music? Remember that you can change the soundtrack in World Cup Ping Pong. There are also three different paddles available, which allow you to make the game a little more personalized to your own preferences and playing style.]

quick review
★★★☆☆

3D Brick Breaker Revolution

Developer: Digital Chocolate, Inc. + **Genre:** Games
Price: $2.99 + **Release:** February 27, 2009

Summary

Breaking bricks has never looked so good, or been so easy. The brain trust over at Digital Chocolate has knocked it out of the park with this Breakout-style game, setting a new bar for the classic formula. Featuring seemingly endless levels and boss battles, 3D Brick Breaker Revolution has a depth that is rare to find in this style of game. Break bricks with over 20 different power-ups, including Nukes, Freeze Shots, and the unstoppable Fury Ball to move through the levels and unlock bonus rounds.

Why we like it

This is truly vintage gaming updated for the 21st century. Breakout was one of the first mainstream video games in homes and arcades, and the formula has remained a staple ever since. 3D Brick Breaker Revolution takes the classic concept and does a great job innovating and refreshing it. With three different game modes and updates that are always adding new levels and power-ups, this one is worth checking out for its depth and 3D graphics, which look great on your screen. It will keep you coming back for its gameplay.

[With 30 different achievements to reach, 3D Brick Breaker Revolution can seem like a console game. Try to earn all 30 badges but remember that some can be challenging. Also, try to unlock all the secret bonus levels: sometimes these two tasks are one and the same.]

Zombieville USA

Developer: Mika Mobile + **Genre:** Games
Price: $1.99 + **Release:** February 15, 2009

▶ Summary

Your town is overrun with the living dead. A lesser person might run, but they're just on the fast track to becoming zombie-fied themselves. You, on the other hand, are going to kick some zombie butt and make heads roll, literally! As the lone survivor of the zombie apocalypse, it's up to you to do battle using 15 different weapons that are all upgradeable. Mow 'em down and pick the change out of their pockets as you battle for survival in this whimsically fun App!

▶ Why we like it

Autosave is such a handy feature that it should come with every game. Zombieville will save your game after each level so you can play at your own pace. The game is simple to play, but its depth will surprise you: with 15 weapons and finite supplies of cash and ammo you need to budget, asset management is an important detail of this game. It's also nice to be able to listen to your own music: just start up your iPod before playing and Zombieville's music will courteously fade out.

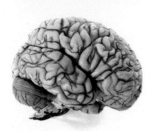

[
  Zombieville looks great—the 2D animations are thoughtful and richly-detailed, and the cartoony look works well. Zombieville is a game that does a lot of the little things right, and that makes for a genuinely fun and original game.
]

quick review
★★★★☆

Touchgrind

Developer: Illusion Labs + **Genre:** Games
Price: $4.99 + **Release:** November 21, 2008

Summary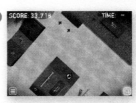

Using the player's fingers as legs, Touchgrind is an innovative skateboarding game that still may be one of the best games in the App Store. Quirky and filled with jumps and other skate park elements, Touchgrind is a great way to pass a few minutes. If the using-fingers-as-legs sounds odd, no worries, it becomes rather intuitive after a few trips to the skate park. Touchgrind also goes fairly deep for an Apps game, featuring video tutorials, competitions and jam sessions that will keep players busy. There are also a multitude of bonus skateboards to unlock which add even more variety to the game.

Why we like it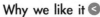

Skateboarding games have been popular for more than a decade, and the innovative use of the touch screen is a feature that no other skateboarding game has. Using the fingers to skate, jump, and perform tricks becomes second nature after awhile, thanks to the very responsive controls, a testament to Illusion Labs' sick App-making skills. Overall, the graphics, controls, and interface are awesome, though it can occasionally be hard to see where the skateboard is going.

quick review
★★★☆☆

MONOPOLY Here & Now: The World Edition

Developer: Electronic Arts ✦ **Genre:** Games
Price: $4.99 ✦ **Release:** December 3, 2008

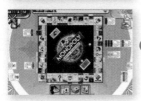

❯ Summary

Classic games really seem to shine on the iPhone and iPod Touch, and Monopoly is no exception. Electronic Arts has packed fun new features inside a familiar package to make the cumbersomely named MONOPOLY Here & Now: The World Edition the latest and greatest version of the venerable game. Shake, swipe, and tap your way to board dominance, competing against the computer or family and friends. You can also rock out to your own music in The World Edition, as it allows you to use your iPod while you play.

❯ Why we like it

It's a classic board game that nearly every person has played. The original dates back to the 1930s, meaning it has durability and universal appeal that few games can match. This version does the game justice, with some clever graphics that help you to enjoy the original game in a whole new way. The game pieces are animated and have their own unique sets of motions, making for a fun user experience. You can also play with up to four players by either passing your device or using WiFi.

[Monopoly is one of those games that's hard to beat in its original, old-school format, but Electronic Arts knocked it out of the park. Make sure you know that since it is the World Edition, the names of the properties will be a bit different, but otherwise it's the same game.]

quick review
★★★☆☆

CLUE

Developer: Electronic Arts + **Genre:** Games
Price: $4.99 + **Release:** May 12, 2009

Summary

The classic board game you know and love has a new user experience on the iPhone and iPod Touch. Who did it? Was it Mr. Green in the kitchen with the candlestick? How about Colonel Mustard in the dining room with the poison? It's all up to you to figure out in this reborn classic. Tap your screen to ask the six original characters questions about their whereabouts on that fateful night, and sleuth through the mansion to find clues as to who murdered the millionaire.

Why we like it

The newly-redecorated mansion looks fantastic on the iPhone or iPod Touch screen. The rooms have been redone by the artists at Electronic Arts specifically for the App, and it has never looked better. Character animations are spot on in this App, and the controls are big and user-friendly. The touch controls allow you to search in cabinets and under furniture, around corners and in the fireplace. Record the clues you find within the App so you don't have to write anything down, and remember that the tips from the editor can often help solve the crime.

[
Unlike the original board game, there's plenty here to keep you guessing right up until the last moment. Look out for the alternate twist endings occasionally thrown in, and pay attention to the body language of suspects. Often times, how they act around you is a clue!
]

Blocked

Developer: Joel Rosenberg + **Genre:** Games
Price: $0.99 + **Release:** August 30, 2008

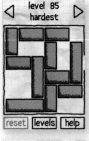

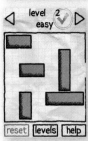

> Summary

Slide the blue block off the board. While that's all there is to Blocked, be forewarned: it gets really tough after a few levels. With three difficulties to make sure you always have the right challenge and 100 levels to play on, Blocked may quickly become one of your favorite games. The objective is to use the other blocks on the board to slide the blue block into oblivion. Sound easy? The goal is very simple but sometimes the blocks can simply stand in your way, offering you no help. You'll have a blast teasing your brain with Blocked!

> Why we like it

There's no learning curve for Blocked: you can begin playing almost immediately. It keeps track of everything you've done in the game, and even auto-saves so you can come back to the same point again. The hand-drawn graphic effects are cool and make it obvious that someone spent a lot of time working hard to make this a truly unique and original App.

UniWar

Developer: XPressed + **Genre:** Games
Price: $0.99 + **Release:** April 27, 2009

Summary

The best online multiplayer strategy game for the iPhone and iPod Touch, UniWar is a turn-based board game based on real-time strategy. Take turns with an opponent building up your armies and fighting against enemy units, utilizing your strengths and taking advantage of changes in terrain. With a 21-mission campaign to go along with the epic multiplayer mode, UniWar is well worth the bang for the buck. The game is also platform-agnostic, so you can play friends who use a different mobile device.

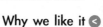

Why we like it

The depth of the online multiplayer is fantastic in UniWar. You'll never tire of playing with friends over WiFi, especially since you can play two against two, three against three, or even more. The regular multiplayer head-to-head is great as well, and the AI of the single player game is also thoughtful and tough. With different game settings and options to go along with the online chat, this game seems to have as much depth as many of the well-known massively multiplayer online PC games.

Games

[A combination of a board game with real-time strategy elements and a little RPG thrown in for good measure, UniWar's fusion of genres makes for a fantastic game to play among friends. One of the few true online multiplayer games in the App Store, it's worth a look.]

Solitaire

Developer: MobilityWare + **Genre:** Games
Price: $0.99 + **Release:** April 23, 2009

▶ Summary

It comes on 90 percent of all computers sold in the world, and it's a fixture on mobile devices and on card tables everywhere, so why not add Solitaire to your App selection? Also known as Klondike, this App is simple yet elegant, featuring the most commonly known rules and options for playing the game. Unlike some other solitaire Apps in the App Store, Solitaire supports drag and drop card movements as well as landscape and portrait mode, allowing the user to decide how they want to orient their device.

▶ Why we like it

It's an old classic but with enough bonus features to keep us coming back for more. The ability to play in landscape or portrait is something that would be nice to see in more card game Apps, and the auto-save feature is nice when you get a phone call or text message that pulls you away from the game. You can draw one or three cards from the deck, score in standard or Vegas modes, keep your statistics, and even auto-complete the game if you think you're stuck with no solution.

[
Tired of looking at the same old card deck in Solitaire? The App supports both custom card decks and custom backgrounds, so feel free to customize both to your heart's content. Also, if you back yourself into a corner, remember that Solitaire has unlimited undo's.
]

quick review
★★★☆☆

UNO

Developer: Gameloft + **Genre:** Games
Price: $4.99 + **Release:** November 14, 2008

Summary

A classic card game that was an obvious App, UNO has been a favorite for generations. The game, of course, is simple: try to get rid of all your cards before your opponent can by dragging and dropping them where they fit. Customize each game with nine different rules settings and be on the lookout for your favorite cards: Wild, Reverse, Draw 2, and many more. UNO has never been this fun or easy to play.

Why we like it

When it comes to playing card games on your iPhone or iPod Touch, there's not one that has a cleaner or better presentation than UNO. The App is speedy, the controls are precise, and the game runs smoothly with no hiccups. The ability to play online with friends via either local WiFi or over the greater internet is a fun option that should be in more Apps. Tournament Mode offers a new and exciting twist in the single player game that gives UNO even more depth and keeps you coming back for more.

Games

[
Think you remember all the rules to UNO? It may have been several years since you last played so be sure to pay particular attention your first game back, because you just might learn a thing or two about this classic.
]

quick review
★★★★★

Texas Hold'em
Developer: Apple, Inc. + **Genre:** Games
Price: $4.99 + **Release:** July 7, 2008

▶ Summary
The most popular casino and card App in the App Store is one of the earliest gaming Apps—and still one of the best. Texas Hold'em is the most popular form of poker: you receive two cards and then try to make the best poker hand from five cards that are drawn for the entire table to use. It takes just a few minutes to learn but can quickly become addictive—and help you understand what all the fuss is about when watching poker on TV.

▶ Why we like it
Just like real players, your opponents will have tells to indicate their standing. Of course, you're not immune to this either: you'll have your own involuntary tells or you can emote using one or two finger gestures on your touch screen. You can play against either realistic AI opponents or use the immense online multiplayer world to find people to play against. With unlimited re-buys and full statistical tracking, Texas Hold'em is worth a look now more than ever.

[Turn your device to switch from the overhead view to first-person. We prefer the overhead view for the incredible speed with which you can shuffle through hands once you get the hang of it. Oh, and the simple secret to winning, is to only play premium hands!]

quick review
★★★☆☆

BlackJack Teacher Pro

Developer: Pepper Stuff + **Genre:** Games
Price: $2.99 + **Release:** June 18, 2009

Summary

Designed to help you succeed in real-world casinos, BlackJack Teacher Pro is much more than just a card game App. It's a full-featured tutor that teaches you how to maximize the odds in your favor when you're wagering real money. With different modes that concentrate on different levels of strategy, this is no simple card-counting instructional. Instead it does things like addressing card combinations that give beginners the most trouble. And since every casino has slightly different house rules, BlackJack Teacher Pro allows you to tweak the rules the tutor is teaching accordingly.

Why we like it

This App doesn't just teach you the basics of the game. Once you get a handle on the rules and understand the generalities of when to bet and how much to lay down, the App really digs deeper in training you to become the best blackjack player you can be. It does feature bet charts for those players that like to have something to consult, but it really hones in on strategy you can learn and apply.

Games

Targeted training with BlackJack Teacher Pro will allow you to focus on your weak areas and make you a better player. The True Count systems are also good to know—though you may never get the chance to use the strategy in the casino, it's a handy skill to have.

quick review
★★★★☆

YAHTZEE Adventures

Developer: Electronic Arts **+ Genre:** Games
Price: $2.99 **+ Release:** November 10, 2008

⊳ Summary

A nice update of a classic, YAHTZEE Adventures brings all the fun of the original dice game plus many exciting new features to the App Store. If you want to just play a quick game of Yahtzee, speed mode lets you jump right in and give it a go from the launch of the App. Throwing the dice is fun, too: give your iPhone or iPod Touch a shake and then tap the screen to score big. Also, if you want to listen to your own music while playing, YAHTZEE Adventures supports your iPod playing in the background.

⊳ Why we like it

Electronic Arts hits all the right notes in this one of their many classic licensed titles in the App Store. Yahtzee has been a commercially popular game for over 50 years, and has become part of the fabric of popular culture when it comes to dice games. This version features four modes including Adventure, Rainbow, Duplicate, and Battle—meaning there's more depth and flexibility to this Yahtzee App than you can find in any physical versions of the game.

[
Think that Yahtzee is just about luck? There's plenty of strategy involved in scoring high point combinations when a Yahtzee is impossible. Try out different methods for scoring the highest points and remember, the odds of a one-spin Yahtzee are roughly one in 22 rolls.
]

quick review
★★★☆☆

FiveOAK

Developer: Clickgamer.com + **Genre:** Games
Price: $0.99 + **Release:** June 17, 2009

Summary

A fun, new, and addictive solitaire dice game, FiveOAK combines your skills and a dash of luck to make a fun App that you'll enjoy for hours. It's designed for one or two players, and the goal of the game is to get the highest score from 13 rolls of the five dice. In each 'hand', the dice can be thrown up to three times, depending on if you like your score or not. If you use fewer rolls, you will score bonus points. The name of the game comes from the most valuable hand, the FiveOAK, also known as a Yacht, which is five of a kind.

Why we like it

It's a twist on both Yahtzee and Solitaire, and since those are two classics, it's cool that developers figured out how to make a fun game out of combining them. With a choice of backgrounds and several customizable options, you have the chance to make FiveOAK look exactly how you want it to. The game also keeps track of your individual statistics and maintains an all-time leader board, so you can see how you stack up.

Games

[
Are you falling far behind? There are many ways to make up points in FiveOAK. If you only use one toss a hand, you can earn more points. If your rash gamble pays off, you'll be rewarded with even more points. Be careful though, because this risky strategy can also bite.
]

quick review
★★★☆☆

Leaf Trombone: World Stage

Developer: Smule + **Genre:** Games
Price: $0.99 + **Release:** April 15, 2009

> Summary

Are you ready to hit the world, or at least the backyard, stage? Step in front of five real-life judges to get their take. The game is easy—make music by following the floating leaves on the screen and slide your fingers accordingly. It's simple, fun, and you'll be playing for hours. The game requires no musical talent to play, and you'll become an expert in no time. Smule's website is also very helpful, and it provides video tutorials for Leaf Trombone.

> Why we like it

This game is unique because you can do two other things besides just play music. Perhaps the most fun, you can judge other players live on their playing. Decide whose performances deserve praise or silence by becoming a judge, but be careful not to be mean! It's you who decides who belongs on the world stage. You might even discover a new talent! If you don't quite have the gumption to play or judge yet, you can simply watch while other players perform and are judged.

> Want to compete for cash? Try out Leaf Trombone's "Feel the Love" contest. Follow the links to Smule's website to enter and have your friends and other fans vote for your performance using either the full version or the free App. The highest rated players will earn cash.

quick review
★★★★☆

Brain Exercise
with Dr. Kawashima

Developer: Namco Networks America, Inc.

Genre: Games ✦ **Price:** $5.99 ✦ **Release:** June 3, 2009

Summary ◂

One of the best brain testing and training games is now on the iPhone and iPod Touch, and it's better than ever. Supervised by Dr. Kawashima every step of the way, you'll test and train your brain like with no other App you've ever used. Scientifically proven and meticulously researched, Dr. Kawashima knows how to effectively challenge the human brain. If you don't have the time to take part in the full training program, try the Quickplay feature to get started. With a great community and support behind it, you'll thank yourself for downloading Brain Exercise.

Why we like it ◂

The Brain Training program stretches, strains and trains your brain like no other App we've ever seen. With a calendar function to keep track of your daily progress, Brain Exercise helps you document your improvements. Bonus content is a plus as well—there are additional levels to be unlocked by progressing through the different exercises, and a new Challenge mode allows you to go head-to-head with a friend. The community aspects are also nice as there's an enthusiastic following on the App's website, and the App has a strong Facebook presence as well.

> Wondering about exactly what you can unlock through your progress? The best is possibly a full-featured Sudoku, which includes three different difficulty settings. Finding out your true brain age is fun, work on your skills to make your brain "younger" or "older".

quick review
★★★☆☆

Lemonade Stand

Developer: Maverick Software ✦ **Genre:** Games
Price: $0.99 ✦ **Release:** March 8, 2009

Summary

A simple and fun economic simulator, Lemonade Stand is both a faithful port of the original Apple II title as well as a much-needed update. You're in charge of running your own lemonade stand and it's all up to you—setting prices, figuring out how much lemonade to make each day depending on the weather and other conditions, even how much to spend advertising your stand. If you want the true oldschool appearance, you can even switch back to the classic graphics of the original.

Why we like it

With every update, Lemonade Stand gets a bit better. The latest version causes more random events to come your way, including parades and conventions. The new Career Mode allows you to play beyond the original App's 30-day limit, so try to see how high you can make it up the leader board. We like how the game can show off its currency in whatever form the user is most familiar with. The old Apple II synthesizer effects are a trip back in time for older players, and the optional classic graphics are just more lemony goodness.

[
With global high scores, you can see how well you stack up against other Lemonade Stand players around the world. The game also features the nifty automatic save and resume that's an essential part of any good App.
]

quick review
★★★☆☆

Toddler Teasers Shapes

Developer: Toddler Teasers + **Genre:** Games
Price: `FREE` + **Release:** January 26, 2009

Summary

When two adults realized that their two-year old toddler could use their new iPhone better than they could, Toddler Teasers was born. With four different quiz games available in the App Store, it's important to say that all of them are worth a look for parents. Shapes may be the gem of the bunch. Allowing your children to concentrate on learning their shapes, Toddler Teasers Shapes won't overwhelm them with information. The game is different every time it plays, so there's no chance of the toddler falling into repetition instead of recognition.

Why we like it

There are many different shapes represented here—in addition to the basic circles, squares and triangles, there are ovals, hexagons, crescents, hearts, and even diamonds. The game will challenge your toddler because it gradually becomes harder, with more shapes being added to the mix every time. You'll appreciate how well this App occupies children, and you might even gain a few extra minutes to do get something done while they're riveted!

After every four answers, your child is rewarded with a sticker. If you and they like Shapes, it's worth trying the other Toddler Teaser Apps, which include a four-pack called Toddler Teasers Quizzing.

quick review
★★★★☆

Bejeweled 2

Developer: PopCap Games, Inc. + **Genre:** Games
Price: $2.99 + **Release:** August 20, 2008

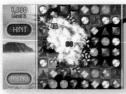

❯ Summary

If you feel like you've seen Bejewled 2 before, you're not crazy. The App is one of the most popular paid games on any platform in the history of mobile gaming. The gem-swapper is simple: you can move a gem one spot per turn. You have to move the gem so the swap lines up three or more gems of the same color, causing them to explode. The more matches you make, the higher your score will go. When you clear a certain amount of matches, the game will take you to a new and more difficult level.

❯ Why we like it

Bejeweled is a modern classic. Like Tetris, it takes seconds to learn but can quickly become an addiction. Sometimes, making a match will leave you without any other possible matches and ends your game—it takes critical thought to be able to think two or three moves ahead. With both landscape and portrait display, Bejeweled 2 has several user-friendly features including allowing users to listen to their own music as they play. The default music is solid too with more than 40 minutes on the catchy soundtrack.

[Matching four in a row ignites a colored gem that will cause an explosion all around it the next time it's matched up. If you manage to score a five-gem match, you get a radioactive gem that will explode all gems of a certain color depending on which color gem you swap it with.]

quick review
★★★☆☆

Supermarket Mania

Developer: G5 Entertainment **+ Genre:** Games
Price: $0.99 **+ Release:** February 26, 2009

Summary

Ever thought about running your own grocery store? Try it out today with Supermarket Mania. Help store proprietor Nikki keep her shelves stocked and her customers happy in a game that has captivated millions of computer users and is now available as an App! Different every time you play, Supermarket Mania has more than 20 accessories you can buy to help out Nikki. Stay tuned for updates from the developers, because a new Endless Mode is coming for players who can't get enough.

Why we like it

As a casual time-management game, Supermarket Mania is much more accessible for the whole family to play than some other games in the category. Simple for non-gaming inclined parents and even younger kids, it's fun for the whole family. The game has depth too, as keeping five stores well stocked is no easy task and there are 50 levels to go through. There are more than a dozen products to sell in your shops and seven different types of customers, so the variations on food and fun are almost endless.

[
If you're a fan of other time management games like Sally's Salon and have a friend that's interested in trying out the same style of game, Supermarket Mania is a good place to start. It's a great introduction to the genre.
]

Games

quick review
★★★☆☆

Scoops—Ice Cream Fun For Everyone

Developer: NimbleBit ✦ **Genre:** Games
Price: $1.99 ✦ **Release:** June 18, 2009

▶ Summary

Scoops—Ice Cream Fun For Everyone is ready to make your kids want to chill. A fantastic App for young ones that aren't ready for more advanced Apps but have outgrown the toddler Apps, Scoops is worth a look for parents. It should occupy your children's interest as the cool colors and airy attitude exude fun. How high can you stack your ice cream cone? Up to the top of the screen? Past the moon? Scoops gets harder and harder the higher your stack goes, so controlling the device with the tilt function becomes a tricky task.

▶ Why we like it

For all its awesomeness as a kids' game, Scoops—Ice Cream Fun For Everyone shines through with some fantastic gameplay. It's got what every good game App should have: simplicity, intuitive and responsive controls, and the all-important ability to play your own music as the game's soundtrack. Local high score boards are available and players have the option of mailing their top scores to their friends to brag about their stacking stature.

[The game might be simple but here are a few hints. Though you should eat them in real life, the veggies in Scoops should be avoided as they don't go well with ice cream. Yuck. Also, try to stack similar colors of ice cream to score even more points.]

quick review
★★★★☆

Pet Playpen

Developer: sparebytes.com + **Genre:** Games
Price: $1.99 + **Release:** June 1, 2009

Summary

Over a decade ago, virtual pets swept into the hearts and minds of kids everywhere. With tiny, hard-to-read, one-color LCD screens, the pets were still unbelievably popular for a time.

Now, thanks to the wonders of technology, an idea that showed so much promise is back in a big way with Pet Playpen. Play, feed, groom and interact with up to five different pets on your screen, caring for them and making sure they're happy in this 'game' that's sure to leave your kids happy. You can adopt up to three pets, which range from the standard dog and cat to the wild penguin or the goofy rock.

Why we like it

Virtual pets have been a neat idea for kids for a long time but they are finally realizing their potential in Pet Playpen. There are over 80 different items that players can buy for their pets, and players can help make the most out of them. There are several fun mini-games to be had as well—Follow the Leader, Frisbee Fetch, and Sledding are just a few of the activities players can enjoy with their pets.

Games

Guitar Rock Tour

Developer: Gameloft + **Genre:** Games
Price: $4.99 + **Release:** November 3, 2008

Summary

Play guitar and drums like a true rock god with Guitar Rock Tour. You don't need to know how to play music to jump right into this App since it takes no experience and about a minute to learn how to play. With 17 of the world's most famous rock songs, you're sure to quickly find something that suits you.

Why we like it

Gameloft clearly spent time trying to make this the best looking App they possibly could and this game boasts awesome graphics, even though they don't need to be on an App like this. Sound is more important in a music App, and Guitar Rock Tour has its tunes down with some of the best audio around anywhere. If you like similar rhythm games, Guitar Rock Tour is certainly worth a look. You may find some of your old favorites and some new tunes to rock out to in a fun and innovative interface.

quick review
★★★☆☆

Tunes Quiz

Developer: refulgentis + **Genre:** Games
Price: $1.99 + **Release:** June 8, 2009

Summary

Think you know the music on your iPod? Tunes Quiz cleverly makes a game out of that existing content on your IPod. The game plays a 10-second clip of a song randomly selected from your iPod, then you have to answer a question about it in 10 seconds. Luckily, the questions are multiple choice, though that doesn't always make it easier. Tracks may sometimes have the song's name included in the beginning, while others may just have a note or two before they really get going, making this an added challenge.

Why we like it

If you have a lot of music, be forewarned: you may not know your tunes as well as you think you do. You'll have to identify the artist, song, or album, and the questions can get challenging! The App does a nice job of presenting you with tough choices, such as having questions about multiple albums from the same artist when asking you about what album a song came from. This App is fun to use and can help you rediscover music you lost track of or just have not listened to in a while.

[Tunes Quiz will keep track of your 10 highest scores and display that info on the screen while you're playing, giving you a target to shoot for. If you lock your device while playing, the game will automatically save itself and return you to the same point when you unlock.]

quick review
★★★☆☆

DJ Mix Tour

Developer: Gameloft + **Genre:** Games
Price: $4.99 + **Release:** June 3, 2009

Summary

Test your rhythm senses in a rocking club environment with DJ Mix Tour. Featuring 16 of the hottest dance tracks ever, including world-wide hits like Sandstorm and Just Dance, there's something new to be mixed every time you play. Choose from one of five different characters to begin Career Mode and you're on your way to becoming a mix master. Never spun before? No problem. DJ Mix Tour is easy for beginners to pick up and you'll be DJ-ing like a pro in no time.

Why we like it

Gameloft comes through again with a solid music App. Like Guitar Rock Tour, DJ Mix Tour has outstanding graphics that make it a benchmark for other music Apps. The four difficulty levels help with players unfamiliar with the style of the game, so whether you're a beginner or a professional DJ, you can jump right in with DJ Mix Tour. The five different locations are all cool and funky, and the 3D animated crowd really comes alive when you're mixing well.

[Use the game's built in Mixing Tool to create your own funky remixes of the game's songs. Mix and scratch on the game's turntables to make your own unique mixes. Be sure to follow the Twitter of the App for new info and updates.]

quick review
★★★☆☆

Name That Guitar Riff

Developer: nuTsie ✦ **Genre:** Games
Price: $0.99 ✦ **Release:** March 20, 2009

Summary

Think you know the greatest riffs in rock history? Put your ear to the test with Name That Guitar Riff. A perfect party or road trip game, it'll have friends clamoring to compete to see who knows the most about guitar riffs. Playing the game couldn't be more simple: Hear a clip of the guitar playing and answer the question afterwards. There are three different levels of question for each riff: Groupie, Roadie, and Rock Star.

Why we like it

This App is easy fun for any music fan. Your friends will love playing with you for hours, and when it was put to the test on a road trip, the App performed admirably for hours without ever becoming boring or repetitive. If you've ever played "Name That Tune" in the car, you'll really appreciate this game. It's also great in a social setting: it's a blast to see friends competing to see who knows the most about the songs being played.

Games

[Do the riffs in Name That Guitar Riff have you aching to hear the whole song? Pick up nuTsie's Mega Music Pack that includes the full version of the songs from the Top 100 Guitar Riffs of All Time, on which this App is based.]

quick review
★★★☆☆

Bloons

Developer: Digital Goldfish, Ltd. + **Genre:** Games
Price: $0.99 + **Release:** April 5, 2009

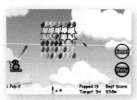

1. Pop it   x 4   Popped: 13   Best Score: Target: 34   93.8x

24. Melting Steel   x 1   Popped: 1   Best Score: Target: 41   82.0x

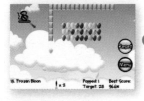

15. Frozen Bloon   x 2   Popped: 1   Best Score: Target: 28   96.6x

Summary

It was a Flash internet sensation and now Bloons is available in the App Store. Using a wide array of darts and special weapons, you're a goofy monkey trying to pop as many balloons as you can. It's simple and hugely addictive; you have to pop a certain number of balloons within a time limit on each level to advance to the next. You'll need skill, luck, and not to mention a bit of magic to keep going as the levels get more difficult. If you lose, you'll be surprised at how quickly you're tapping "New Game" to give Bloons another go.

Why we like it

Bloons is the best kind of puzzle game: easy to play yet captivating. The variety of Bloons is fun, as there are ice bloons, tack bloons, helium bloons, and bomb bloons, among others. You'll never get tired of Bloons, either. There are 100 levels, many of which are exclusive to the App Store version of the game. When you've exhausted these options, there's also a level editor that lets you design your own challenges.

quick review
★★★☆☆

iRings

Developer: Fonware, Ltd. + **Genre:** Games
Price: $1.99 + **Release:** June 19, 2009

Summary

Requiring lightning-quick reflexes along with your tilting and tapping skills, iRings gets your brain working hard from the start. It's a puzzle game that's based on the arranging of colored rings, and the objective is to arrange the colors horizontally, vertically, or diagonally to score. The more rings you manage to clear, the more points you earn. Online leader boards let you compare your iRings scores with others. Do you think you have what it takes to be the best?

Why we like it

You needn't have the nimblest player in the world to succeed at iRings. The game will adjust to your playing speed. Some players prefer faster speeds because it means more rings will come their way. But there's an advantage to going slower—you have time to think and be sure you're making the smartest moves possible. It's nice to have that element of strategy in a simple game. The 3D graphics look sharp and the in-game music matches the pace of play well.

[The controls to iRings are fun and intuitive. It will take a combination of using the tilt functions on your iPhone or iPod Touch and tapping the screen to maximize the scoring potential of your rings]

quick review
★★★★☆

JellyCar

Developer: Walaber + **Genre:** Games
Price: FREE + **Release:** October 20, 2008

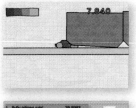

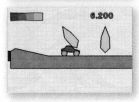

❯ Summary

One of the most popular kids' games in the App Store, Jelly Car has been critically acclaimed for its original gameplay. A driving game and a platform game combine to make a puzzling challenge. JellyCars is all about squishy cars navigating through a squishy world. With soft body physics in play for every item, the goal is to simply squeeze through to the end of each level. You'll have to think quickly and creatively to clear the board.

❯ Why we like it

It's fun, addictive, and not just for kids. Adults can also get behind the wheel in JellyCar, making the game fun for all. With cool, seemingly hand-drawn graphics, JellyCar is also a beautiful App to look at. It's simple to play—just tap your finger the way you want to go, tilt your device, and off you go. There are no difficult maneuvers to make, though you can briefly trans-form your JellyCar by tapping on it. If you think you're not seeing everything clearly, pinch zooming is a cool feature (it should be added to more games).

Having trouble navigating through parts of a level? Try tapping the question mark for some How-To instructions on the game in general, or remember that your JellyCar can transform for a few seconds to help you wiggle and wrangle through a level.

quick review
★★★☆☆

Topple 2

Developer: ngmoco, Inc. ✦ **Genre:** Games
Price: $2.99 ✦ **Release:** March 11, 2009

Summary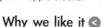

With over 30 levels in six different Topple worlds, Topple 2 is a worthy sequel to its downloaded-by-millions predecessor. Gameplay is the same concept as the original: stack colored Topple blocks and try to not be the one that makes the whole tower go tumbling over. There are several new modes to master in Topple 2, including the world-changing Upside Down Mode, which flips your idea of Topple right on its head. Balance Mode lets you weigh two towers against each other; Power Mode challenges you to build a power line using blocks; and Rescue Mode calls on you to protect the Golden Egg with your Topple blocks.

Why we like it

With all the new modes, levels, and worlds, there's so much to love about Topple 2. The visuals look great, and like the first game, Topple 2 features an awesome and sweeping musical score to accompany play. Fully utilizing the tilt and tap controls of your device, Topple 2 does a great job of making it all seem effortless. There's so much in Topple 2 you'll never be without a new challenge—this title will keep you occupied for a long time.

Perhaps the coolest new feature of Topple 2 is being able to face your friends in "Stack Attack" mode in real time. If you're looking for new friends, online multiplayer will match you up with someone new to play or create a "ghost" to face you.

quick review
★★★☆☆

Myst

Developer: Cyan Worlds **+ Genre:** Games
Price: $5.99 **+ Release:** May 2, 2009

▶ Summary

The PC hit from the 1990s has never played or looked better than on the iPhone or iPod Touch. The complete worlds of Myst are all here in their original beauty, and no matter where in the world you may be now, you can carry the Myst world with you in your pocket. If you're returning to the game for the first time in years, you'll be amazed at the improvements.
If you've never played Myst before, you're in for a treat with the fantastic story and tough puzzles of this surreal world.

▶ Why we like it

Everything you remember about the original is here, and the controls of the iPhone and iPod Touch seem made for Myst, as everything feels natural and crisp. The mobile version cuts no corners—all the original music is here as well as the video scenes and animations. Auto-zoom even remains intact. Best of all is the auto-save feature—if you get lost in the world of Myst and get a phone call, your game will save itself so you can come right back to the same spot.

Myst as an App is very big: about the size of a movie and clocking in at over 700 megabytes. Make sure you have the space available for the game before you download. If you have the space, however, give it a try since Myst is one of the best puzzle adventure games ever made.

quick review
★★★★☆

Toobz

Developer: Off Center Software **+ Genre:** Games
Price: $0.99 **+ Release:** April 19, 2009

Summary

A challenging game with a quick pace, Toobz forces you to think on the fly as you make decisions and plan moves in a race against the clock. The goal is to create a series of pipes throughout the level, beginning from a random point. Your Toobz must all connect and flow freely without spilling any water. As you progress, the time you get to complete each level will decrease, increasing the mental challenge of Toobz. Featuring four difficulty levels but also with a time-limit-free mode, there's a pace to suit everyone's needs.

Why we like it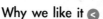

It's a classic game in a new, sharp-looking package. It's also tough to play—if you let in any water there are no re-dos, you have to start all over again. The two game modes, "Classic Toobz" and "Show Toobz" each provide a unique twist to the game and increase its replay factor. A nice function is the automatic pausing of the game if you get a phone call, meaning you can return to the same spot once you're done yapping.

Games

> Think you've got Toobz beat? Turn the water on as soon as you think you have a completed network. If your gamble pays off, you'll be rewarded with a time bonus heading into the next level. Take a few seconds and check your work, you don't want to have to start all over.

quick review
★★★☆☆

Enigmo

Developer: Pangea Software, Inc. + **Genre:** Games
Price: $2.99 + **Release:** June 17, 2009

Summary

An awesome new gravity-based puzzle game, Enigmo is a simple idea that gets twisted in fun and wacky ways. It is up to you to direct streams of flowing liquid down each level so the drops reach their destination. You'll be playing with water, lava and oil as they move down each level. Move an array of bumpers, sponges, accelerators and sliders to divert the flow of the droplets so they reach the right destination, and you'll receive bonus points if you're able to do it quickly.

Why we like it

Enigmo has surprising depth. With 50 levels, it's hard to get bored with this App. The physics were designed to be as accurate as possible so be careful when moving around the objects within the level since the liquids will react according to their viscosity. The best part of Enigmo, however, might be the bonus levels. With a home computer version already out on the market, there's a wide array of levels already created by other Enigmo players. You can download them for free, meaning you'll never run out of new things to try!

[If you're looking for the cream of the crop of the user-created levels, try purchasing Level Packs within the game. The store is a new feature in the latest edition of Enigmo, and selecting the upgrade is easy if you want to take a look at these exclusive add-ons.]

quick review
★★★☆☆

Bookworm

Developer: PopCap Games, Inc. ✦ **Genre:** Games
Price: $4.99 ✦ **Release:** March 8, 2009

Summary

Think you're a bookworm? You don't have an appetite like Lex the Bookworm. Join him on an adventure through letters, linking tiles left, right, up and down to make words. Each word will help keep Lex happy and satisfied, but pay attention to the red-hot burning blocks, since they spell trouble for both you and Lex. Remember that the bigger the word, the more nourished Lex will be. Keep trying to string longer words together, but remember to not over think and to keep it simple when you need to in this fun and lighthearted game.

Why we like it

It's educational and crazy fun at the same time. The game is easy to learn for players of all ages, and every mode is accessible from the beginning for new players. Words can be simple or vocabular building; it's all about what you're able to find in the puzzle for Lex to gobble up. Stat tracking is simple but works well to keep high scores and there are enough bonuses for working faster and finding bonus words to keep players entertained well beyond the first few plays.

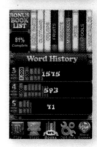

Games

[Feeling a bit stuck and needing a new perspective on the game board? Shake your iPhone or iPod Touch—this will scramble the letters and/or give you a whole new set of letters to link up for Lex.]

quick review
★★★★★

Need For Speed Undercover

Developer: Electronic Arts **+ Genre:** Games
Price: $6.99 **+ Release:** April 27, 2009

❯ Summary

Featuring 20 of the world's fastest cars doing what they do best, Need For Speed Undercover is the latest revolutionary title in the NFS series. It will wow you with the graphics and pace: no other iPhone or iPod Touch game moves like Undercover does. The white-knuckle racing action has fantastic drift handling, and every car is customizable to the style of the player. The game features a sound-track by up-and-coming hard rockers Airbourne, but gamers can add their own soundtrack using their iPod.

❯ Why we like it

The Need for Speed series is one of the most respected names in racing, and Undercover is no exception to this elite lineage of racing games. Undercover is just as deep as any of its console brethren—beyond the 20 customizable cars, there are eight game modes which include several Need for Speed classics like Highway Battle and Cop Takeout. With three different environments and 24 covert missions, Undercover seems impossi-bly huge for an Apps game. The action is fast, but the controls are crisp enough for precise driving.

[Looking to gain that little something extra while on the run from oppo-nents or the police? Swipe your finger to activate the Nitro Burst and Speedbreaker to quickly bounce away from your pursuers. To rule the road, be sure to avoid obstacles like signs and other cars.]

quick review
★★★★☆

2XL Supercross

Developer: 2XL Games, Inc. + **Genre:** Games
Price: $7.99 + **Release:** April 1, 2009

Summary

An all-new off road racing game from the experts in asphalt racing, 2XL Supercross is an exciting relative newcomer to the App Store. A rhythm-based racing game, 2XL Supercross is easy to learn, but the challenges increase as you play. You'll have to navigate through treacherous jumps, hoops and turns while trying to beat your opponents, which is no easy task. Not sure if you're ready to take the plunge? 2XL also has a Lite version available so you can ride before you buy.

Why we like it

The tracks in 2XL Supercross were designed by moto and supercross star Stephane Roncada, and his knowledge of the sport shows in the layouts of the tracks. It's fun to see how your times stack up worldwide, so login to the 2XL server and post your times. You can even share this great game with friends because 2XL Supercross allows you to create five different gamer profiles within the App.

[The three different modes of play in 2XL Supercross also allow you to race in three different classes: 125cc, 250cc, and 450cc. The game will also automatically adjust the number of opponents you race against based on the optimal settings for your device.]

quick review
★★★☆☆

Space Shuttle

Developer: Laminar Research + **Genre:** Games
Price: $1.99 + **Release:** May 6, 2009

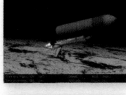

⊙ Summary

Think you can make it as an astronaut? Space Shuttle cuts no corners in giving you the full experience you might get if you were to fly with NASA. From the 10-second countdown before launch, to docking with the International Space Station, to returning back home, Space Shuttle lets you do it all. Re-entry starts from about 600 miles out and you have to glide the shuttle all the way home to Edwards Air Force Base from Mach-10 at an altitude of 200,000 feet. Think you have the right stuff? Space Shuttle demands your best, and will reward you if you can accomplish your mission.

⊙ Why we like it

Space Shuttle is intense but is not for everyone. It takes dedication, patience, and a strong will to successfully complete missions, and we appreciate that. If you can make it through the launch sequence, there's still the challenge of docking with the ISS. You have full control along six different planes and the geometry of the real shuttle and space station are represented accurately, so precision is key. Re-entry is difficult as well, and landing is frighteningly fun since you're controlling the shuttle like it's the real thing.

quick review
★★★★☆

Line Rider iRide

Developer: inXile Entertainment + **Genre:** Games
Price: $2.99 + **Release:** September 9, 2008

Summary

If you can draw it, Bosh will try to ride it! A boy on sled, Bosh is at the mercy of you, the artist behind his run. He'll try to go down any run you throw at him, no matter how many twists, dips, or jumps you deviously put in his path.

His run is only over when he gets to the end or wipes out. It's a simple concept that yields great fun, and you and your friends may never tire of sending Bosh down your runs.

Why we like it

This App is both straightforward and attractive. It's a simple concept and the graphics are about as basic as can be. Even young children can draw a run for Bosh and it's simple enough for any adult to get the hang of in a minute or less. This is truly a unique game for everyone, and although you aren't racing against anyone, you'll still find yourself captivated by this quirky title.

Games

[
Think your creation was pretty cool? Upload your masterpieces to inXile's servers and see how others measure up. You can even download and rate tracks created by others, browsing by the highest-rated or most recent runs, or even search for them by their creator
]

Fast & Furious The Game

Developer: I-play + **Genre:** Games
Price: $5.99 + **Release:** April 2, 2009

▶ Summary

Based on the hit blockbuster action movie, Fast & Furious is much more than just another movie tie-in game cashing in on a license. Dominate the racing scenes of Los Angeles, Mexico and the Dominican Republic, making sure not to lose your ride or worse if you fall behind. Try to dominate the world of Fast & Furious with online multiplayer mode, which pits you against thousands of other players at any one time, but be sure not to lose your car in "Pink Slip" mode.

▶ Why we like it

Showcasing impressive depth and stunning graphics, Fast & Furious is one cool game. The accelerometer controls work like a dream and make this an easy game to pick up and play. Updates keep making the game better. You can post your best times to Twitter and show off to friends, see if you can top your own custom leader boards, or challenge other players' best times on a run with YouTube-enabled Ghost Runs. There's so much to do in Fast & Furious that you'll spend hours trying to drive through it all.

One of the most realistic driving games available from the App Store, Fast & Furious features 36 different cars across a wide range of styles including classic American muscle cars, top European exotics, and tuned-up Japanese customs.

quick review
★★★☆☆

X-Plane Extreme

Developer: Laminar Research + **Genre:** Games
Price: $9.99 + **Release:** January 29, 2009

Summary

From the top name in iPhone and iPod Touch flight simulators, X-Plane Extreme is a crazy and incredibly deep simulator of some of the coolest aircraft flying today, featuring some of the most expensive beasts to ever take flight. Players can take control of the B-1 and B-2 Bombers, the SR-71 Blackbird spy plane (the fastest plane ever built), and the F-22 Raptor. With incredibly realistic controls, just keeping these planes in the air is a victory in itself at first, but you will soon be flying like an Air Force pilot.

Why we like it

Few developers pay as much attention to detail as Laminar Research. For example, if you fly at night you can look up at the stars as they appear in the nighttime sky, but don't take your eyes off your instruments for too long. From being parked on the runway to flying at 100,000 feet, X-Plane Extreme lets you control the entire flight. With realistic aeronautics and controls, you can't get closer to flying than X-Plane Extreme, so try out each plane's unique attributes and choose your favorites.

[Just like in real life, every plane handles dramatically differently, so learning how to control each aircraft will take time. Kudos to the developers for the exceptional authenticity!]

quick review
★★★☆☆

Moto Chaser

Developer: Freeverse, Inc. ✦ **Genre:** Games
Price: $0.99 ✦ **Release:** July 4, 2008

❯ Summary

One of the original racing games in the App Store, Moto Chaser remains one of the top sellers because it's still one of the best. With thrilling high-speed action blasting your bike through richly-detailed 3D environments, steering is a breeze with accelerometer-based controls. To battle with opponents, simply tap the screen to try and shoo them out of your way. Leap extreme jumps and twist the throttle to try and cross the finish line first in this fun and addicting arcade racer.

❯ Why we like it

If you played 16-bit video games, you'd be familiar with the Road Rash series of motorcycle racing games. Moto Chaser takes its inspiration from the classic series, so if you liked those games, you'll love this updated take on the formula. Having controls for both arcade and simulation style racing is a nice touch for gamers who may have different preferences. This title has won numerous awards, deservedly so in our opinion.

[Worried about rival bikers coming up from behind you? Make sure you're paying attention to the road ahead of you. Danger in the form of obstacles or new enemy riders could be lurking just around the next bend. Don't forget to tap your screen to wipe them out!]

quick review
★★★☆☆

Mindracer Duel

Developer: Spielhaus + **Genre:** Games
Price: FREE + **Release:** June 8, 2008

Summary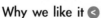

A racing game can come in all shapes and sizes, and there might not be a more unique racing title in the App Store than Mindracer Duel. Unleash your basic math skills with fury as you race to beat an opponent to the right answer. The faster you're able to tap in the correct answer to the question, the faster you'll move. Racing glory is... a few math problems away?! You can practice on your own and hone your basic math skills, but it's more fun to play against someone.

Why we like it

This App is great for a few laughs but it's also fantastic for parents with young kids. They can race against mom and dad while working on their math at the same time, and it's even more fun for them when they're able to beat their folks to an answer and win a race. Problems are randomly generated and there's plenty of variety. This game is a keeper because it's fun and educational—a rare combo.

> With a small memory footprint and a price that can't be beat, it's definitely worth the time to check out Mindracer Duel. It's a ton of fun to play with a friend and the full version will remain free until the developers write a lite version, so pick it up ASAP!

Games

quick review
★★★★☆

Baseball Superstars

Developer: GAMEVIL, Inc. ✦ **Genre:** Games
Price: $2.99 ✦ **Release:** June 4, 2009

❯ Summary

The top-selling baseball game in the App Store and one of the bestselling role playing games as well, Baseball Superstars is a must have for any fans of the game. It's great for casual players looking to have a good time by taking a few swings, but really shines when played by hardcore baseball fans. It's just like the real deal if you've ever imagined being a Major Leaguer, but with some twists. You create your player and you control everything: his look, gear, and even training.

❯ Why we like it

This game has a ton of depth and some awesome unlockables, including 12 new players. With 10 different teams and four different stadiums, there are always new variables to keep the game fresh. The modes are deep—beyond a regular game and season, players can compete in My League, Home Run, or Mission mode. Taking your player through the ranks is fun, and there's no other baseball game out there that allows the customization detail that Baseball Superstars does. And with the ability to swap out your player's gear, there's no shortage of fun you can have with your new player and franchise.

> If you like Baseball Superstars and are also a fan of other sports, GAMEVIL offers deep, RPG-style simulation sports games for hockey, football, and basketball. They love sports and it shines through in their roster of MVP-caliber titles.

quick review
★★★☆☆

ZENONIA

Developer: GAMEVIL, Inc. **+ Genre:** Games
Price: $5.99 **+ Release:** May 24, 2009

Summary

ZENONIA has an estimated 40 hours of playing time—a staggering amount for an iPhone and iPod Touch RPG—to help get you through even the longest commute. It harkens back to classic RPGs of the past but looks like a modern handheld RPG title. The top-selling RPG in the App Store, ZENONIA features anime-style characters and graphics and a solid storyline, which makes it reminiscent of Nintendo's fabled Zelda franchise. It's gotten rave reviews with good reason—RPGs are rarely this deep from the App Store.

Why we like it

If you're clamoring for a classic RPG experience, you need to look no further. Plop down the six bucks for ZENONIA and revel in oldschool RPG goodness. It has a 17-item skill tree for character development, hundreds of unique items for each playable character, item classes, and a day/night cycle that really shines. Without giving away too much of the story or being too linear, it also features an alternate storyline dependent on whether or not you decide to do good or evil deeds. With other innovative elements along with the hallmarks of a classic RPG, fans of the genre should consider downloading this one.

> The controls of ZENONIA are exceptional, featuring an on-screen D-pad to maneuver through the world. Picking it up and playing is easy as using your device. You will automatically turn to face your enemies, and the touch screen is a nice asset when doing battle.

Games

quick review
★★★★☆

Rise Of Lost Empires

Developer: Gameloft **+ Genre:** Games
Price: $4.99 **+ Release:** June 3, 2009

❯ Summary

Centuries of peace have come to an end and Hell's Gate has been thrown down, leading to the rise of the Empire of Darkness. The next great war is unavoidable, and it's up to you to choose a side and lead your Empire to ultimate victory. With more than 20 missions in each campaign and over 20 units and buildings on each side, you'll constantly be challenged to gain an advantage over your computer opponent. Optimized for the touch screen, controlling your Empire is easy, but the missions are not.

❯ Why we like it

Being able to play in either campaign with Humans or Orcs provides a fun element that enhances the replay factor of Rise Of Lost Empires. The ability to add one of six great heroes to lead your armies is an extra challenge when you're fighting against an opponent who has one. The graphics are fantastic—light and cartoony at times, everything is exceptionally detailed and it's easy to see what's going on in the game. The medieval music provides a cool soundtrack to the game.

It's a tried and tested formula, pitting Humans against Orcs. It's worked for many years, and Rise Of Lost Empires is a fun and intuitive expansion of the concept. The controls are fantastic so navigating through the beautiful environments is a snap.

quick review
★★★☆☆

Underworlds

Developer: Pixel Mine, Inc. + **Genre:** Games
Price: $0.99 + **Release:** May 8, 2009

Summary

One of the premier action/adventure-RPG games on the iPhone platform, Underworlds features a thrilling quest with a fantastic story. As the guard of a traveling caravan, it is your job to protect against occasional raiders until a mysterious attack looms on the horizon. You'll face wicked leaders and terrible enemies roaming among the living, and it's up to you to defeat them all. Hack and slash your way through the game, but you'll also have to master the healing arts to make sure you're always in top fighting shape. As you improve, your enemies will become more difficult to defeat, but you'll also improve.

Why we like it

The gory gameplay is fun and exciting, but it's the subtle nuances that players must pay attention to. If they ignore the healing arts for instance, they will never survive long enough to unleash their full offensive fury. The depth of the story really balances well with the need for constant improvement in your player to make an overall fun gaming experience.

Games

Unlike other games that are ports from older games or designed with other mobile platforms in mind, Underworld was solely designed for play on the iPhone and iPod Touch. The controls are fully customizable for either a right- or left-handed player along with a directional pad.

quick review
★★★☆☆

iBox

Developer: Tractus Design + **Genre:** Games
Price: $0.99 + **Release:** June 18, 2009

> Summary

The latest update to iBox has made the pugnacious App deeper and more fun than ever. Train for a bout using your iPhone or iPod Touch by tapping the heavy bag and speed bag. Other drills are there too—practice with the punching mitts, work on your shadow boxing, and jump rope to improve foot speed and get the most out of your training. Make sure to snap your wrists like in a real punch to get the full sound effect of each movement.

> Why we like it

The extra features are a ton of fun, especially the Ring the Bell game that comes straight out of carnival midways. Turning on the crowd ambiance when boxing also helps give it a realistic feeling, and if you need a longer or shorter round break to recover, that option is customizable. The physics are cool as well. iBox can accurately display the power and speed of your punches, including the all-important pounds per square inch. While the game is incredibly fun to play, it's the attention to detail and the inclusion of little extras like these that make it a champion.

[
If you're looking for an even bigger challenge than the already sweat-inducing iBox, turn the App to Expert Mode. It decreases your device's sensitivity, making it harder to get the result you're looking for, especially in mini-games like Ring the Bell.
]

quick review
★★★☆☆

WarShip

Developer: Goorusoft + **Genre:** Games
Price: $1.99 + **Release:** May 26, 2009

Summary

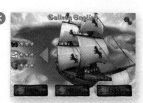

Ready to risk life and limb sailing the high seas? Then WarShip is the ocean-going exploration sim for you. Try to discover new lands that humans have never laid eyes on, but you must always be vigilant. The high seas are a dangerous place and there's always the threat of violence on the horizon. With powerful enemies in each zone, it takes a master tactician to successfully navigate in WarShip. As you survive assaults, your ship becomes stronger, but be sure to always be on the lookout for pirates.

Why we like it

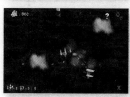

A unique and original App, there's nothing else out there like WarShip. The challenge of defeating enemies in every sector of the sea is something would-be ship captains will relish, and will soon find themselves sucked into the swashbuckling. The defeat of each enemy ship adds a special feature to your WarShip, which helps you become Master of the Seas. But watch out for pirates! They will come and try to steal your trophies, which adds an element of realism that sailors have to face on the high seas even today.

[Be sure to save your money for a new warship. If you can, try to hold out as long as you can with your current ship. Make sure to grab any trophies that your enemies have dropped into the water, as they can become valuable tools in your quest to rule the oceans.]

quick review
★★★★☆

SimCity

Developer: Electronic Arts **+ Genre:** Games
Price: $4.99 **+ Release:** March 4, 2009

❯ Summary

A classic that everyone knows and loves the original SimCity being brought back to action by Electronic Arts. The predecessor of every Sim game that's followed, including its direct sequels, spin-offs like SimAnt and hugely popular game franchises like The Sims, SimCity still stacks up well against its newer brothers. The original city management game, SimCity challenges you to make use of a limited budget to create a city teeming with active Sims. As your city thrives, you'll generate more money to improve roads, add services, or make the city bigger.

❯ Why we like it

Though it's a version of the original game, SimCity has never looked better than this port. Big buttons make it easy to navigate the options for first-time players, and if you've played the game before, you'll be able to quickly step right back in and start your newest creation. The best of the original is all here—road and rail, power plants, and residential and commercial districts. With three different difficulty modes, starter cities, and tutorials for new players, SimCity is accessible to everyone.

[If you're bored with waiting around and want to see how well your city can withstand the worst that Mother Nature has to throw at it, introduce a natural disaster. There are fires, tornadoes, earthquakes, toxic clouds and even UFOs.]

quick review
★★★★☆

Ouch!

Developer: Hondune Games ✦ **Genre:** Games
Price: $2.99 ✦ **Release:** March 15, 2009

Summary

A truly open-ended game, Ouch! centers on throwing your own customizable ragdoll through level after level of obstacles and objects. Score points at the end of each level based on how much damage your ragdoll took. By simply tilting your device to move the ragdoll around as gravity takes its hold, Ouch! is easy to play and is fun for all ages. Try to cause more damage by interacting with objects on the screen like pinball flippers, cannons and cars.

Why we like it

With over 45 scenes to play through, Ouch! has surprising depth and replay value. All of the customization options are fantastic for making your ragdoll truly your own. With over 65 props to hit and otherwise interact with, there's always something amusing going on the screen. The physics are also as realistic as possible and response is great. Ouch! also includes a full-featured level editor to make your own levels, and since every level in the game was built with the same editor, you can truly create your own game-caliber levels.

Games

Want to make your character look like yourself or a friend as you toss it through the levels? Use the camera on your iPhone or preloaded pictures to customize a ragdoll.

quick review
★ ★ ★ ★ ★

Real Soccer 2009

Developer: Gameloft + **Genre:** Games
Price: $2.99 + **Release:** September 8, 2008

❯ Summary

It's the most popular sport in the world, and now you can play one of the deepest sports games available for mobile devices on your iPhone or iPod Touch. Real Soccer 2009 has all the latest rosters and star players, making it ready to tackle any other mobile soccer game. With cool touch screen controls and trick moves along with awesome tilt-screen throw-ins, you're likely to discover something new every time you play Real Soccer 2009.

❯ Why we like it

Multiplayer mode over WiFi is seamless and fast, making it easy to compete against a friend in Real Soccer 2009. One of the most awesome features is the FIFPRO license the game carries, allowing it to have the real players for 198 teams. With 12 stadiums, there's surprising depth that's not seen even in some console soccer titles. The graphics may not be as good as some of the other soccer titles out there, but they're respectable. Touch screen controls also work well but this title still really shines thanks to its incredible depth. You almost won't believe the volume of options the first time you boot it up!

When it comes to finding a well-rounded sports game, look no further than Real Soccer 2009. The game looks great, controls great, and has amazing depth. There might be flashier-looking games out there, but none shoots and scores like Real Soccer 2009.

quick review
★★★☆☆

Streetball

Developer: Battery Acid Games + **Genre:** Games
Price: $1.99 + **Release:** February 4, 2009

Summary

The cool graphics of Streetball make it unique from the start. It doesn't try to pull off 3D like other sports games. Instead, it relies on cool 2D drawings of highly detailed players with neat animations to make its own graphical impact. Play tight defense to trap your opponents or just swat their shots away to get the ball. On offense, take jumpers from the outside or drive to the hole for a thunderous dunk, all using the touch screen. Tap your screen to shoot, pass, block and dunk your way to hardwood heroics.

Why we like it

If you only get one basketball game for your iPhone or iPod Touch, make it Streetball. While the earlier versions may have struggled with a lack of depth, the current version has evolved into an all-star. The controls have been tweaked to make your players more responsive than ever, and new characters mean you now have six types to choose from. The new accuracy bar also helps you decide whether or not it's time to shoot. And for the hardcore competitors out there, the High Scores board lets you compete against friends (or your own scores) to see who is king of the court.

[Do you like the newly added High Scores feature in Streetball? Want to know how well you stack up against other players? Stick with the App: an update has delivered an interactive leader boards for all to see who the best ballers really are!]

quick review
★★★☆☆

Flick Fishing

Developer: Freeverse, Inc. ✦ **Genre:** Games
Price: $0.99 ✦ **Release:** November 6, 2008

❯ Summary

Flick Fishing is the top fishing simulator in the App Store, with an intuitive interface and richly detailed fishing environments. Controls are a snap: just flick your wrist to cast your line using your choice of bait and tackle, and hope to land a fish. If you do, it's time to reel in. Just be careful not to snap your line, as big fish will fight hard and not come into your boat easily. With a wide array of fish and fantastic detail, Flick Fishing is well worth a dollar.

❯ Why we like it

It's unrivaled as a fishing simulation in the App Store. There are eight different locations to fish, nine types of bait and tackle, and 12 different tournaments to compete in. And for the fish: there are dozens of different species to catch. The controls are great and this game is just good, plain fun. The multiplayer is also fantastic: play head-to-head over a network against a friend or trade off turns in Hot Seat. When you catch the big one, you can even brag to your friends via e-mail!

The newest version of Flick Fishing contains some great updates to the game. There's a new fishing location available for purchase and you can also catch three new types of fish. Be sure to also try Fish Jack—it's a network blackjack game within the App, but with fish.

quick review
★★★★☆

Tiger Woods PGA TOUR

Developer: Electronic Apps ✦ **Genre:** Games
Price: $6.99 ✦ **Release:** April 23, 2009

Games

Summary

The world's top golf video game is now in the App Store and lets you feel like you're really on tour with Tiger Woods. Swipe the screen with great precision to shape the shots you want using the game's spin control, and follow each stroke using interactive cameras. You can use players like Tiger Woods, Vijay Singh and Retief Goosen or take the course with some of the top women's players like Annika Sorenstam and Natalie Gulbis.

Why we like it

It's a bit pricier than most Apps, but worth it for the level of detail you get in this game. EA SPORTS are masters at getting sports games right, and this mobile version of Tiger Woods PGA TOUR features real golfers and 120 holes of championship golf spread across seven of the world's best courses. Pebble Beach and St. Andrews make this a must-have game for any golf fan. And the live play-by-play commentary from real life broadcasters Sam Torrance and Kelly Tilgham is an added dose of realism.

[
Remember that you don't have to play as Tiger in the game. You can also try to beat him, but be forewarned, he's the best in the world. Enjoy hearing the crack of the clubs and the cheers of the crowd as you climb to the top of the leader board.
]

quick review
★★★★☆

The Sims 3
Developer: Electronic Arts + **Genre:** Games
Price: $9.99 + **Release:** May 29, 2009

⟩ Summary
The desktop classic is making its debut on the iPhone and iPod Touch, and it looks great. Enjoy endless hours of fun as your created Sims live their lives in a world you create. You give your Sims their personalities: Shy, Funny and Bored are just a few of the many options. You control how they look as well, from their hairstyles to their clothes. Pick a fight or make friends, be nice or mean, torture or treasure your Sims, it's all up to you!

⟩ Why we like it
With surprising depth, The Sims 3 can quickly captivate. With 73 goals and wishes for your Sims to achieve, there's always something to aspire to. It can be hilarious as well, as some of the more eccentric Sims will knock over garbage cans and even talk to trees. And since it is among the biggest games in the App Store, you can truly lose yourself in the town your Sims live in. The circle of life is virtually infinite in The Sims 3—there is no ending so you can enjoy endless hours of fun.

[You can help your Sims meet their goals and dreams or not. It's all up to you. The accelerometer and touch screen get great applications here, as they are used to maneuver your Sim through the richly-detailed 3D world.]

quick review
★★★☆☆

Brain Teaser

Developer: Uwe Meier **+ Genre:** Games
Price: FREE **+ Release:** May 30, 2009

Games

Summary

Be forewarned: Brain Teaser is not easy. At the bottom left of your screen is a pattern of tiles with a certain color pattern and your goal is to simply match the pattern on the screen. But you won't be shuffling tiles around; instead you'll be flipping them over with a tap of the screen. The difficulty comes with the effects of a flip—all neighboring tiles will flip as well. You have a limited time to solve each puzzle, making it a race to complete as quickly as possible.

Why we like it

Because it's so darn tough, finishing puzzles in Brain Teaser can give you quite a sense of accomplishment. It's so simple to learn that anyone can play. In fact, it almost sucks you in with its simplicity before confounding you with its complexity. The level of difficulty increases gradually and the first few puzzles are easy. The game forces you to think creatively as you are required to remember patterns for some puzzles—while forgetting about patterns to solve other puzzles. Your mind will definitely get a workout from Brain Teaser, and it can even help jumpstart creativity.

[Is Brain Teaser awesome but simply too hard with the time clock? The newest update of the game has been getting rave reviews thanks to its option to turn off the timer.]

quick review
★★★★☆

Sally's Spa

Developer: Games Café, Inc. ✦ **Genre:** Games
Price: $0.99 ✦ **Release:** April 8, 2009

❯ Summary

Get treated to some spa fun and relaxation in Sally's Spa. The top time-management game in the App Store, Sally's Spa is fun for all. Take control of spa owner Sally and manage your salon, such as dealing with customers and expansion. With 65 different items available to spend your hard-earned money on (including new employees), there's always something to work for. With great graphics and seamless use of the iPhone and iPod Touch's touch screen, controlling Sally is super easy.

❯ Why we like it

This game is at the top of the list for both paid and free Apps in Strategy for a reason—it's one of the best. While the free version is fun in itself, it's worth a buck to get the full-fledged App. There is no other time-management game like it, whether in the App Store or anywhere else. Cute and yet strangely addictive, Sally's Spa has all the features of the Mac and PC editions packed into the App. With 50 levels and 10 different locations, there's almost endless variety.

[On the surface, Sally's Spa seems like a simple game aimed at girls, but it's a great game that is fun for kids and adults of both genders and of all ages.]

quick review
★★★☆☆

The Oregon Trail

Developer: Gameloft + **Genre:** Games
Price: $4.99 + **Release:** March 9, 2009

Summary

Go West, young man! The classic
westward exploration game is back
and better than ever on the iPhone
and iPod Touch. Featuring all-new
mini-games and side missions to go
along with the classic strategy of the
original, this incarnation of The Oregon
Trail may be the best. After you select
your party and stock up for the trip,
try rafting, wagon repairing, telegraph-
ing, panning for gold and berry picking.
But be on the lookout for hitchhikers
and bandits who may cross your path
when you let your guard down.

Why we like it

Many people may recall playing
this game on computers in school
when they were young, so there's a
nostalgia factor when firing up The
Oregon Trail for the first time. The use
of the touch screen and accelerometer
make hunting and river crossing more
fun than ever, and new mini-games
and side missions give the game even
more depth. Plus the game is not only
fun, it's educational as well.

[
It may look different than the game of old, but The Oregon Trail still has
the same challenging elements it has always had. Be sure to remember
to take care when fording rivers, and watch out for the illnesses that
can wreak havoc on your wagon train.
]

quick review
★ ★ ★ ★ ☆

Wheel of Fortune

Developer: Sony Pictures Television ✛ **Genre:** Games
Price: $4.99 ✛ **Release:** February 27, 2009

❯ Summary

Spin the Wheel, pick a letter or buy a vowel, and solve the puzzle in this awesome adaptation of the classic television game show. The game is fun, exciting, and if you're lucky, you might even land on the $1,000,000 wedge. Including over 1,000 puzzles from the television show and original puzzles as well, there's so much variety here that you'll never get tired of spinning the Wheel! Featuring the familiar theme music and sound effects you already know and love, Wheel of Fortune makes you feel like you're a contestant.

❯ Why we like it

You can't go wrong with a little Wheel of Fortune every now and then. The game show has been on television so long because it's fun and people love shouting answers at their screen. This App transports you squarely into contestant's row, where you have to pick the letters and compete against the clock and other players to solve the puzzle. Pop-up tutorials help beginners and the game rewards players with trophies for various achievements.

[
This App's developers clearly put a lot of time and love into making what is perhaps the best game show game in the App Store. In fact, the producers of the television show worked on the puzzles and helped design the game to make it feel as much like the real thing as possible.
]

quick review
★★★☆☆

Trivial Pursuit

Developer: Electronic Arts ✦ **Genre:** Games
Price: $4.99 ✦ **Release:** April 23, 2009

Summary

Get your piece of the pie with the classic Trivial Pursuit. Featuring thousands of questions in each of the six classic categories, Trivial Pursuit is an update of the vintage trivia game. You can battle friends or the computer in Classic and Pursuit Mode. The App uses the power of the iPhone and iPod Touch as well: shake the device to roll the dice, swipe your way through categories and tap your way to the right answers. View statistics when your game is over to see what percentage of questions you answered correctly.

Why we like it

This is the ultimate party game since you can play with four players on just one device. Having multiple game modes is always a plus—it helps to have different ways to play a game, meaning you'll spend more time with the App. The variety of questions is vast, and the picture questions add an element to the game not seen in the actual board game. It's also nice to be able to skip your opponent's turn if you don't want to watch all of the animations.

Games

Trivial Pursuit shines with its customization options. You can make your player look like you, a monkey, or even a pirate if you like. You can also set up the game to suit your preferences—select the number of wedges it takes to win and how much time you have to answer each question.

quick review
★★★☆☆

Jeopardy!

Developer: Sony Pictures Television + **Genre:** Games
Price: $4.99 + **Release:** April 3, 2009

> Summary

One of the greatest game shows in television history, Jeopardy! shines on the iPhone and iPod Touch. It's packed with over 2,000 questions set in 360 different categories, so you will rarely encounter the same question twice in Jeopardy! Thanks to challenging questions along with the iconic music and graphics of the TV show, you'll feel like you're there. The original introductions from the show are intact and give Jeopardy! that extra element of realism to go along with the Daily Doubles and Final Jeopardy that are so familiar to viewers.

> Why we like it

Many attempts have been made to translate Jeopardy! from television to the video game realm over the last 20 years, but it has never been this good. The clues in home editions never seemed to be on par with the real show, but this has been negated in this version by the fact that all the questions come from the actual writers on the show. With the customizable characters and the ability to use the touch screen to write your name how you want, you can really immerse yourself in Jeopardy!

[If you struggle with giving your answers in the form of a question when following Jeopardy on television, don't worry about it with the App. Every question is multiple choice and the game offers three different levels of difficulty.]

quick review
★★★☆☆

Movie Challenge

Developer: Electronic Arts + **Genre:** Games
Price: $4.99 + **Release:** April 23, 2009

Summary

Think you know your movies? The full version of Movie Challenge will test your smarts with over 5,500 original questions about the big screen. Try out the free version, Movie Challenge Lite, first to try out the App and answer over 300 questions. With great graphics and sound effects, Movie Challenge Lite offers five categories, three difficulties, and three different game types. With a bustling community of players, Movie Challenge Lite may quickly become your favorite trivia game.

Why we like it

With its anti-repetition settings, Movie Challenge Lite provides maximum variety even though the free version has fewer questions. Updates for the regular and frequent question packs are free even with the free version of the App. The developers provide their e-mail address for direct feedback, which is always appreciated, and best of all, the game saves automatically, so when you have to leave Movie Challenge Lite you can come right back to the point you were at.

Games

Having trouble learning how to play Movie Challenge Lite? Tap your way over to the How To Play section for detailed instructions. It will cover all of the topics in the game and make it easy to pick up and play.

quick review
★★★★★

SCRABBLE
Developer: Electronic Arts + **Genre:** Games
Price: $4.99 + **Release:** July 9, 2009

> Summary
The granddaddy of all word games, SCRABBLE in the App Store is the full version of the classic title. Featuring one-on-one or head-to-head battles over WiFi, there's always someone to play with. Shake your device to shuffle letters, zoom in and out on the board, and just drag and drop to place tiles. With flexible difficulty levels and score-tracking for leader boards, it's easy to find the right challenge for any player.

> Why we like it
It's a classic, but now you never have to worry again about losing those dang tiles. The "teacher feature" is also a fun way to get better, as it displays the word that would have been your best play on a previous move. Another major bonus comes for users with Facebook. As long as your friends have SCRABBLE on their profiles, you can play against them from your iPhone or iPod Touch.

[
Want to play with friends who are on Facebook but don't have an account? SCRABBLE will help you create a Facebook account so you can connect with friends! The interface improves with each update, so try out Facebook Connect with SCRABBLE today.
]

quick review
★★★★★

Cheat Codes

Developer: Prima Games **+ Genre:** Games
Price: $9.99 **+ Release:** January 26, 2009

Summary

With 50,000 codes, cheats, tips and tricks for over 4,000 games on each major console, Cheat Codes is a must-have for all video game enthusiasts. Packaged neatly in an easy-to-use browse or search interface, Cheat Codes is brought to you by Prima Games, the most trusted name in video game strategy. No company devotes more time to making video games more accessible for everyone, so you can count on Cheat Codes to help you get the most of your game library.

Why we like it

As the world of video games evolves, Cheat Codes is in lock-step. Constantly updated with the latest titles and newest discoveries from games already in release, users who download this App can be sure that if a code is uncovered for the Xbox 360, PlayStation 3, Wii or Virtual Console, it'll appear in Cheat Codes. You can also save your favorite titles and read up on the latest video games news in the App, making it a one-stop destination for gamers. Plus, every trick in, or uploaded to, the App is first certified by the gurus at Prima Games.

[Looking to finish a game to 100% completion or wish you could find all of a game's hidden Achievements? Look up the game in Cheat Codes, where you can find all of the Achievements for a game as well as tips for accomplishing the goals!]

The New York Times Crosswords Daily 2009

Developer: Magmic, Inc. + **Genre:** Games
Price: $5.99 + **Release:** March 6, 2009

> Summary

Missing the king of all crosswords? Pick up The New York Times Crosswords Daily 2009 App. It's the premier crossword puzzle in the world wrapped up in one awesome package. Write in "pen" or "pencil" as you work to solve crosswords in the fastest time possible. With clue hints and highlighting of related clues, you can even get the crutch you need to solve the crossword. The same puzzles that appear in the New York Times each day appear here, so you never have to worry about missing another crossword!

> Why we like it

It's not just a simple crossword puzzle that pops up on your screen every day, it's a full-featured crossword App. The game includes access to an archive of crosswords dating back to the beginning of the year, but that's not all. The archive also includes over 4,000 historical crosswords from the paper's archive, meaning you'll never be bored. The letter and clue hints are always helpful, and the App also integrates interestingly with the newspaper by providing a view of the front page that day.

[
The community aspects are great. Want to see how good you are against other crossword solvers? Check out the online leader boards and compete for the best times. You can also send messages and compare your solving times with your friend's.
]

quick review
★★★☆☆

Free Hangman

Developer: MobilityWare + **Genre:** Games
Price: FREE + **Release:** June 13, 2009

Summary

Hangman is a classic game that nearly everyone knows how to play—try to guess a hidden word letter by letter. If you guess a wrong letter, part of a stick figure is drawn. If it's completed, the player loses the game. Simple but addicting, this game is great if you have a few minutes to burn. And by helping you learn new words, it's educational too!

Why we like it

If you don't know the meaning of one of the words you've been trying to solve, you can tap on the question mark to find out the definition, which can help expand your vocabulary. There's no shortage of words to be found in Free Hangman with 18 different word lists to choose from. You don't have to stare at the same boring background the whole time either: there are five different graphical themes to choose from. Two-player mode is fun as well, as it's always a pleasure to stump family and friends.

Games

[Though this App is full-featured, it is ad-supported. To get rid of the ads, upgrade to the full version. The developers of the game are always looking for suggestions and make their Twitter page available for users to send in ideas for improvements.]

quick review
★★★★☆

iFitness

Developer: Medical Productions ✛ **Genre:** Healthcare
Price: $1.99 ✛ **Release:** June 3, 2009

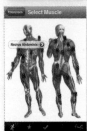

❯ Summary

Exercising regularly is the only way to get your body into shape and to keep it that way. Even people who exercise often, however, may find themselves falling into a dull routine. If you're looking for new exercises or more information about that new lift you heard or read about, then you should check out iFitness. With a comprehensive database of over 200 exercises and 10 pre-set workout routines, iFitness can put a new spin on your approach to fitness.

❯ Why we like it

iFitness has a full set of instructions for every exercise in the App, including full color pictures. It is a great tool for people who are either new to exercise, fitness fanatics, or even physical trainers looking for fresh ideas. Being able to track your performance from each workout and check out graphs can be great inspiration, and the ability to e-mail your workout results lets you break down your performance later. You can even create multiple custom workouts to keep track of different gym days.

[Not sure how long you should be taking between sets? Use iFitness's built-in stopwatch to calculate how long you've been resting. The App also has a built-in weight monitor so you are motivated to keep those numbers on your scale moving in the right direction.]

quick review
★★★★☆

WebMD Mobile

Developer: WebMD **+ Genre:** Healthcare
Price: FREE **+ Release:** October 30, 2008

Summary

The most trusted name for online detailed medical information, WebMD is making its database of knowledge freely available on the iPhone and iPod Touch. Want to know what certain symptoms could mean? Need information about a prescription or over the counter drug? Need basic first aid information? WebMD has all of this plus more. From the most mundane to the toughest emergencies, WebMD has the knowledge to tell you more about a problem in a clear and concise way that most people can understand. With features about treatments including natural methods, WebMD lets you research to help make more informed post-diagnosis choices with your doctor as well.

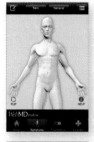

Why we like it

Whether you're concerned about symptoms or just have a basic first aid question, WebMD makes the information easily accessible and palatable for the public. There's very little medical jargon here, just informed and straightforward language. The App is well organized, even when compared to the website. Personal profiles make the App even more user-friendly, and it also allows you to go back to information you might have been accessing earlier without requiring you to re-enter all the symptom data.

[The latest version of the App is the most polished and accessible yet, and new improvements include a clickable body users of the website will be familiar with. Just tap the screen of your device on the body part affected to see a list of possible symptoms.]

quick review

Survival Pocket Ref

Developer: Double Dog Studios + **Genre:** Healthcare
Price: $0.99 + **Release:** May 30, 2009

Summary

If you need to know exactly what to do in an emergency situation, you want to have a reference you can trust. Featuring the exact copy from the United States Department of Defense's Survival, Evasion and Recovery manual, Survival Pocket Ref features the important information you hope you never have to use but should know just in case. With topics as wide-ranging as basic first aid and building a fire to getting drinkable water and navigating by a compass and the stars, this App is packed with no-nonsense info.

Why we like it

In the unfortunate event that you'd need it, this App can be truly indispensible. If you learn some of the skills outlined in the App, you improve your chances of surviving trouble unscathed. The 250 pages cover a lot of material, and actually make for interesting reading on a plane or commute, so don't be surprised if you start browsing and quickly become engrossed!

[The App isn't all just nuts and bolts. The search feature works very well and can quickly guide you to what you want to know. Though reading a government manual originally written for the military can get a little dry, there's a bit of humor mixed in as well!]

quick review
★★★★☆

Diet & Exercise Assistant

Developer: Keyoe, Inc. ✦ **Genre:** Healthcare
Price: $9.99 ✦ **Release:** June 17, 2009

Summary ◐

Looking for a tool to track your progress on reaching your weight loss goals? There may not be a more comprehensive App for that purpose in the iTunes Store than this one. Tracking what you eat, how you exercise, and how far you've progressed towards your goals, Diet & Exercise Assistant helps to keep you in control of your weight loss plan. Select a built-in diet plan or create your own in conjunction with your doctor, and input food and exercises from a fully customizable database of over 10,000 items and exercises, including popular restaurant items.

Why we like it ◐

Diet & Exercise Assistant has existed for several years on other platforms, so the underpinnings of the App are strong; it's seen several revisions and is remarkably polished for a recently released App. Everything that users of the App liked on other platforms is here, made better with new features and the slick interface the iPhone and iPod Touch bring. The blood pressure monitor and body measurements are well-thought out options that are unique to this App. The weight chart is also handy: it tells you exactly where you stand in comparison to other people your height and age, letting you know if you're underweight, normal, overweight or obese.

[Not sure how many calories you're burning? Diet & Exercise Assistant can calculate it all for you! Just enter the exercises and how long you did each for, and in partnership with what the App knows about you, it will figure out exactly how many you burned.]

quick review
★★★☆☆

RunKeeper Pro

Developer: FitnessKeeper, Inc. ✚ **Genre:** Healthcare
Price: $9.99 ✚ **Release:** June 30, 2009

❯ Summary

Are you a runner, biker, hiker or casual walking enthusiast looking to keep exact tabs on where you're going and what you're doing but don't want to spend a ton of cash on special shoes or tracking devices? Use your iPhone 3G or 3GS in conjunction with RunKeeper Pro to track precise statistics about your exercise. Using your device's GPS, RunKeeper Pro will tell you how far you've moved, how long it's taken you, your average pace and much more. You can track elevation changes while skiing or trying a hilly route, and even plot where you've been on a map.

❯ Why we like it

For anyone who participates in outdoor activities with any seriousness, RunKeeper is almost a must-have App. Not only is it simple to use—just press Start and Stop and the App automates the rest—it goes beyond the iPhone interface as well. You can upload your workout results to the web on runkeeper.com and track the results from every time you've used the App. You can also share what you've been doing with friends via e-mail, Facebook, Twitter and many other social networking sites.

> Want to know how well you're moving during your favorite activity? The App can tell you the vital stats of your workout, including pace, time elapsed, and total distance, through your earbuds without making you have to look at the display.

quick review
★★★☆☆

Yoga STRETCH

Developer: Neil Harris ✦ **Genre:** Healthcare
Price: $0.99 ✦ **Release:** November 2, 2008

Summary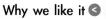

Would you like to improve your mental health, physical strength, flexibility and posture? Start yoga without having to take a class with Yoga STRETCH. Whether you're a complete beginner or a veteran of the Vinyasa flow, Yoga STRETCH has a routine for you. Featuring full audio instruction, music and images designed to maximize your personal abilities and mentally relax you, this App can help transport you to a more peaceful place. Featuring over 60 poses and variations to go along with a customizable plan that can go from a minute to an hour, Yoga STRETCH has something for everyone interested in the ancient art.

Why we like it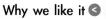

It's much more than a list of moves. The images and vocal instruction in Yoga STRETCH can really help you get each pose right. Yoga STRETCH's instructor isn't just a mindless voice telling you what to do, however, as each pose has detailed information, including the Sanskrit name and a full description of the mental and physical benefits. You can skip through poses you can't perfect yet and go back to poses you've already done, a handy feature that lets you focus on positions that suit you.

> Frustrated at not being able to do some of the poses in Yoga STRETCH? No worries! Remember that yoga is an art that can take a lifetime to master. With every session, even the creakiest body will gradually become stronger and more flexible.

Apps Capsules

❯ Couch to 5k

Developer: Felt Tip, Inc. **✦ Genre:** Healthcare
Price: $1.99 **✦ Release:** May 26, 2009

Using interval workouts, Couch to 5k will have you ready to race in just nine weeks. With voice prompts to coach you and featuring an increasing level of difficulty, Couch to 5k can help boost anyone's fitness.

❯ Pound A Week

Developer: Norfello Oy **✦ Genre:** Healthcare
Price: $0.99 **✦ Release:** June 15, 2009

Keeping track of your calorie intake and usage, Pound A Week strives to help you lose that much weight every seven days. The App also features a large database of both food items and exercises you can do.

❯ aRelax Sound sleep Pro Ambient

Developer: Linloole **✦ Genre:** Healthcare
Price: $1.99 **✦ Release:** June 14, 2009

Having trouble falling asleep? Try turning on some ambient noises to help you relax and drown-out outside or unfamiliar noises. It's fast and easy to use, and you can customize your favorite sounds to make your own ambient noise playlist.

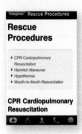

❯ American Medical Aid

Developer: Creative Coefficient Corp.
Genre: Healthcare **✦ Price:** $2.99
Release: June 11, 2009

Faced with a perplexing medical emergency and not sure what to do? Featuring color illustrations and easy to follow directions, the App includes one-tap access to calling emergency services for help.

Find A Hospital

Developer: iHealth Ventures, LLC + **Genre:** Healthcare
Price: $0.99 + **Release:** June 11, 2009

Stuck in an unfamiliar area and need to find a hospital? This App will help you find a hospital near you by using your device's location tracking ability. Features one-tap calling and website access.

Two Hundred Situps

Developer: Software X + **Genre:** Healthcare
Price: $1.99 + **Release:** April 23, 2009

Are you serious about building up your core strength? Whether you can do one or 100 situps, Two Hundred Situps only takes about 30 minutes a week plus your discipline to complete.

Baby Dreams

Developer: Jakub Koter + **Genre:** Healthcare
Price: $0.99 + **Release:** June 2, 2009

Having trouble getting your baby to fall asleep? Is your baby waking up in the middle of the night? Try playing Baby Dreams on a Dock to help them sleep like, well, a baby. The App uses scientifically proven binaural tones.

Stress Reducer

Developer: Ethan Productions + **Genre:** Healthcare
Price: FREE + **Release:** January 3, 2009

Need to relax or unwind and get rid of stress? Select a picture of a shell you like and hold it up to your ear. You'll hear relaxing ocean tones that will deliver serenity now!

quick review
★★★☆☆

Shopper

Developer: Midcentury Software + **Genre:** Lifestyle
Price: $0.99 + **Release:** May 26, 2009

▶ Summary

Ready for a whole new shopping experience? With smart lists in Shopper, you'll never have to worry about forgetting something at the store again. Creating a list of the items you need is just the start—you can shop for items using a smart search function, use old lists as templates for new ones, add notes and photos to your lists, and much more. Shopper will also help you keep organized at the grocery store and on other shopping runs based on what aisle in the store your items are in.

▶ Why we like it

More than just a grocery list aggregator, Shopper gets points for its overall utility—you truly can use it for anything. Having the auto-complete in the lists is a big time saver and convenient if you don't know how to spell an item, like Worcestershire sauce, for instance. Type in the first four letters and it will auto-complete, saving you time and frustration. Displaying both unit price and total price when breaking down the cost of your shopping spree is handy as well. It's also nice to be able to e-mail lists and track prices for the same item from different stores.

[Shopper is a very nifty App that offers a lot of nice extras. It's especially convenient when you have more than one destination, as Shopper knows when you're getting close to a store on your list and will shuffle your lists accordingly.]

quick review
★★★☆☆

Amazon Mobile

Developer: Amazon.com + **Genre:** Lifestyle
Price: FREE + **Release:** April 14, 2009

Summary ❮

It's more than just the world's largest online bookstore. Amazon.com has branched out into selling just about everything, and now that buying power can be yours wherever you are with Amazon Mobile! You can search, browse, create wish lists and buy anything from the App, making it a true one-stop shop. Want access to all of your purchases from the past, user settings, your wish list and cart? Simply log in using your Amazon account and all of your web settings are there.

Why we like it ❮

It's all the buying power of Amazon packed into a handy App. The App is fast, attractive, and easy to use. Anything you can buy on Amazon.com, you can buy via this App. Amazon Mobile also allows you to comparison shop with thousands of online retailers. One-touch ordering is convenient, and being able to track purchases from the minute you place your order to when they arrive is handy and easy to do.

Amazon Mobile contains a great new feature called Amazon Remembers. If you see something you like while out and about, take a picture of it within the App. Amazon will try to track down the item and if they find a match, they'll e-mail you!

Whole Foods Market Recipes

Developer: Whole Foods Market, Inc. **+ Genre:** Lifestyle
Price: FREE **+ Release:** June 17, 2009

▶ Summary

Want to eat healthier? Whole Foods Market is one of the fastest-growing grocery chains in the country because stores are dedicated to bringing higher quality foods to market. They sell only quality meats and produce, but making it all taste good together is up to you. If you want help from a place you already know and trust, it's all about the Whole Foods Market Recipes App. With so many options to choose from, you'll have no problem whipping up something tasty in no time.

▶ Why we like it

The App is well thought out and super easy to use. It handles dietary restrictions like gluten allergy and vegetarianism in a snap, eliminating what can't be eaten with just one tap. Being able to enter multiple specific items is great when you have a typical fridge of random stuff but no idea what to possibly make—the App will incorporate as many of your items as it can and come back with some delish dishes. With nutritional information and full preparation and cooking instructions, this is one of the best recipe managers out there.

[Want to know where a Whole Foods Market is located? Use the Store Locator within the App to find the stores nearest you. You can link to the store's web page and view information such as hours and what foods are currently on sale.]

quick review
★★★☆☆

eBay Mobile

Developer: eBay, Inc. + **Genre:** Lifestyle
Price: FREE + **Release:** September 19, 2008

Summary

Want to browse for everything from cars to chairs to baseball cards? Buy, sell, track and leave feedback for all of your items using eBay Mobile. It's everything about eBay all in one place—if you can do it on the website, you can do it on eBay Mobile. Handling time-sensitive information and setting alerts are a snap as well, and you can browse through hundreds of listings at a time to find whatever you want.

Why we like it

If you're an avid user of eBay, you'll love the main My eBay screen—we actually like it better than the page on the website. With big, bold buttons, the App tells you what you're watching, what you're bidding on, what you've won or lost, what you're selling and the status of the items you're selling. Simply tap any of these to go to a list of those items. Great for both buyers and sellers, this App comes with everything an eBay user could want. From first listing to final payment, eBay Mobile has you covered.

eBay Mobile can update in real time on WiFi networks, meaning you don't have to be in front of your computer to squeeze in that final, winning bid. If you pay using the App, all information is transferred over eBay's secure servers.

quick review
★★★★☆

How To Videos from Howcast.com

Developer: Howcast + **Genre:** Lifestyle
Price: FREE + **Release:** October 6, 2008

Summary

Ever want to learn how to do something new but have no idea where to start? Need to learn how but are too proud to ask for help? Howcast is coming to your rescue! The internet's top destination for high-quality how-to videos, Howcast's free App is a must if you need to learn something in minutes. With lists of editor's picks and carefully organized playlists of related instructional videos, let Howcast teach you something new, and then get lost browsing related content. You'll become an expert in no time!

Why we like it

Howcast has videos on how to do almost anything. If you want to learn how to tie a bow tie, poach an egg, or even make an origami swan, Howcast can teach you how, every step of the way. Howcast helps you to organize your favorite videos with some thoughtful features. Naturally there's an option to create a list of favorites, but if you've forgotten to bookmark a video or just want to go back and see another video again, there's a full History feature to go back and see any video you've ever watched.

Want to know more about a video? Tap the arrow twice within your search results to bring up a more detailed description. Not sure what you want to learn about? Shake your device to bring up a random video from among Howcast's favorites.

quick review
★★★☆☆

Grill Guide

Developer: dadoo + **Genre:** Lifestyle
Price: $0.99 + **Release:** March 16, 2009

Summary

Have your favorite meats or veggies marinating while the grill is warming up, but not sure what to do next? Grill Guide is your cheat sheet for everything you need to know about great grilling. With 95 different cuts of meat included in the App and more available soon, Grill Guide can help you be a better cook. Once you choose your cut of meat, Grill Guide takes you the rest of the way. It will help you measure your cut, tell you how much heat to use, even where to place your meat on the grill.

Why we like it

Perhaps the hardest thing to master in grilling is the relationship between heat and time—how long will it take to cook your food properly, and how hot should the grill surface be? Short of measuring the temperature of the cooking surface, Grill Guide does all the work for you. The interface for measuring the meat by holding your device up to it is handy and fun to use.

Apps Capsules

❯ Control4 My House

Developer: Control UI ✦ **Genre:** Lifestyle
Price: FREE ✦ **Release:** November 16, 2008

If you have any sort of home automation, from one room to your whole house, you need to get Control4 My House. It works with several versions of Control4 to run your home gadgets.

❯ CraigSearch Free

Developer: PheedYou, Inc. ✦ **Genre:** Lifestyle
Price: FREE ✦ **Release:** December 1, 2008

CraigSearch Free puts the power of Craigslist in your hands with its powerful search tool. The easy-to-use interface allows you to search any of the United States Craigslist sites.

❯ DoGood

Developer: Mobile33t, LLC ✦ **Genre:** Lifestyle
Price: FREE ✦ **Release:** June 7, 2009

What happens when millions of people perform the same random act of kindness every day? DoGood flashes a new act for users to do every day, and you can simply click "Done" once it is complete.

❯ dexknows

Developer: Dex Media, Inc. ✦ **Genre:** Lifestyle
Price: FREE ✦ **Release:** March 24, 2009

Looking for something locally? Dex knows the answer. Featuring a search of your local business listings, people search, and auto-locate, Dex has a quick response time for questions about places near you.

Wired Product Reviews

Developer: CondeNet + **Genre:** Lifestyle
Price: FREE + **Release:** November 4, 2008

Need to know about the latest and greatest tech gadget (other than your iPhone of course)? Make sure it's worth your while by looking it up on Wired Product Reviews. New hands-on reviews are added daily.

1001+ Best PickUp Lines

Developer: MacPhun, LLC + **Genre:** Lifestyle
Price: $0.99 + **Release:** June 1, 2009

Looking to start a conversation with someone but unsure of where to begin? Stumbling to find the right words to even say hello? Try out 1001+ Best PickUp Lines, with something new and fresh for any situation.

Blurb

Developer: Yodel Code + **Genre:** Lifestyle
Price: FREE + **Release:** May 15, 2009

Using Blurb you can turn your iPhone or iPod Touch into a scrolling message center to broadcast a large-font message to the people around you. Great for finding people in crowds or at concerts!

Munch

Developer: Avantar, LLC + **Genre:** Lifestyle
Price: FREE + **Release:** May 17, 2009

Know what you want to eat but not sure what's around you? Munch is a must-have if you're looking for a restaurant in a new place. Munch auto-detects your location and finds the best places near you.

quick review
★★★☆☆

Epocrates

Developer: Epocrates + **Genre:** Medical
Price: FREE + **Release:** January 22, 2009

> Summary

Do your eyes unavoidably glaze over when learning about your medications? Want to know what's going into your body and how the different medications interact with each other? Check out Epocrates, a top reference for prescription drug information. A very useful database that can help you and your doctor make confident decisions, Epocrates can help inform the discussion of your treatments. The App has a big database so loading can take a minute or two, but there's so much information here it's worth it if you need it.

> Why we like it

With information on more than 3,300 drugs, the free version of Epocrates has just about everything that the home user needs to know. You can examine the interactions of up to 30 drugs at one time, identify your pills at home to make sure you have the right medication, and perform calculations for things like body mass index when trying to figure out how many milligrams of an over-the-counter medication to take. The jargon can be a bit overwhelming, but there's so much essential info here it's hard to pass up if you or a loved one takes several different meds.

While the free version of Epocrates is stocked with great info, the paid version also includes disease information and ideas for medications that may be substituted for others. While it won't make you a doctor, the info in Epocrates can certainly help you talk to yours.

quick review
★★★☆☆

Memory Matrix

Developer: Lumosity ✦ **Genre:** Medical
Price: $1.99 ✦ **Release:** April 19, 2009

Summary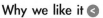

Working out your mind is just as important as working out your body—you need to keep exercising your mental faculties to stay sharp. Memory games can help, as they force you to flex your analytical mind to solve problems and remember patterns, and can boost your memory. Train your brain and stay sharp with this simple memory game that begins with nothing more complicated than a grid of blocks on the screen.

Why we like it

This is possibly the best memory game in the App Store. Simple, fun and easy to use, it's yet another great App from Lumosity. Staffed by medical professionals and scientists, Lumosity knows what makes the brain tick, and their Apps are well-designed and backed by clinical research, so you know you're getting a quality product from them. This App is quick, easy to load, and takes seconds to learn so even if you only have a few minutes, you can still squeeze some skill into your skull.

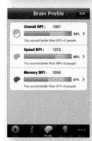

Medical

Want to add a bit of competition to Memory Matrix? Play against a friend and see who's sharper! Competing against someone else is a great way to motivate both of you to improve.

quick review
★★★☆☆

Relax with Andrew Johnson

Developer: Michael Schneider **+ Genre:** Medical
Price: $2.99 **+ Release:** June 15, 2009

> Summary

After a hectic or particularly stressful day, relaxation might be the only thing on your mind, or the furthest thing from your thoughts. Either way, it's important to take a deep breath, slow down and relax once in a while. Feel the pace of your world slow with Relax, brought to you by world-renowned clinical hypnotherapist Andrew Johnson. Whether you need to relax after a long day at the office or can't sleep at night, Relax can help put your mind at ease.

> Why we like it

If you've never had relaxation therapy before, this App will teach you some basic techniques for unwinding. Even for experienced users of meditation techniques, there is benefit to using this App. It is simple but still remarkably effective, and better relaxation can become a possibility for just about everyone. Just hit the big Begin button and feel the world melt away. The newest version has added options in the settings menu and an upgrade in the audio quality.

[If relaxation therapy seems a bit odd for you, then this is the most accessible way to try it out. It doesn't get any simpler than with Andrew Johnson, whose best-selling mp3s and CDs have helped hundreds of thousands of restless souls make more of their down time.]

quick review
★★★☆☆

Total Baby

Developer: ANDESigned ✦ **Genre:** Medical
Price: $4.99 ✦ **Release:** July 3, 2009

Summary

If you're a new parent, keeping track of everything from doctor visits to feeding schedules can be a real challenge. Make it a little easier on yourselves with Total Baby, an App designed to log all of the important information you need to remember about your little one. Featuring a day calendar outlining all of your baby's information for the day, Total Baby will let you know when it's time for a feeding, a nap, or even when your baby has a doctor's appointment coming up. With timers and a diary to help track everything you need to remember, Total Baby helps you better take care of the ones you love the most.

Why we like it

If you have more than one child, especially twins, Total Baby is perfect. In fact, it was designed with parents of multiples in mind. In addition to the basic tasks like Feeding, Baths and Naps, you can add your own custom tasks, such as Medicine and Temperature for when your baby is feeling under the weather. Being able to keep track of doctor visits is also handy, since it can be hard to keep track of what shots happened when.

[Want to see just how fast your young one is growing? Keep track with the Diary, where you can records your child's growth and even add a picture for each entry. Total Baby can keep track of up to six children at a time.]

quick review
★★★☆☆

Quit Smoking Now with Max Kirsten

Developer: Origin Creative ✦ **Genre:** Medical
Price: $7.99 ✦ **Release:** November 16, 2008

> Summary

With thousands of success stories the world over, Max Kirsten's renowned hypnotherapy is one of the more popular ways to quit smoking. His programs have received media coverage and many celebrity endorsements, and now the program is available on the iPhone and iPod Touch. With videos and high quality audio recordings, there are several different aspects to the program, all covered in full in this App. There are also smoking fact cards, letting you know how your progress has helped your body. For roughly the cost of a single pack of smokes, you can start on the road to being smoke-free!

> Why we like it

Quit Smoking Now is a recognized program in the smoking cessation industry, and it's very thorough. The audio in each session—Getting Started, Quit Smoking Now and Booster—is high-quality, and the soothing beats will not only help you quit, they'll relax you as well. The Quit Smoking e-book is a great companion read to go along with the App, featuring information about the program and about quitting in general. The fact cards will help encourage you each day, and the smoking calculator lets you know how much you've saved by quitting.

> [Help to curb your cravings and anxiety while avoiding unwanted weight gain. It's a comprehensive program, focusing on all aspects of quitting, not just the stopping of the physical act. And the thousands of success stories will convince you that it is possible to quit.]

quick review
★★★☆☆

Dream Psychology
by Sigmund Freud

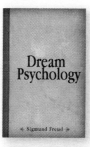

Developer: Appsessions, LLC + **Genre:** Medical
Price: $0.99 + **Release:** January 1, 2009

Summary

The key work of Dr. Sigmund Freud and the cornerstone of dream analysis, Dream Psychology has helped experts and laypeople alike analyze their dreams for more than a century. Both easy to digest and very thorough, this well-designed, compact and concise tome is a bedrock of modern psychology and is a must-read for any student or person looking to learn more about themselves and their dreams.

Why we like it

It's not an audio book or e-book, it's both! It's always nice to be able to read or listen to the book, and you can even listen to it while following along in the text to grasp some of the tougher concepts. If you choose to have both options on, you can have the App automatically scroll as you read along in portrait or landscape mode. In addition to being well designed, Dream Psychology is a classic in the field of dream analysis and Dr. Freud is one of the most renowned authorities on the topic.

With fantastic content and multiple ways to digest the information, the Dream Psychology App is the easiest way to absorb this Freudian masterpiece. Using a wonderful English translation of the original book, Dream Psychology has never been more accessible.

Apps Capsules

❯ Emergency Info

Developer: iHealth Ventures, LLC ✚ **Genre:** Medical
Price: $0.99 ✚ **Release:** June 10, 2009

Keep track of your emergency medical information with Emergency Info. Make sure you never get caught again without the important phone numbers, allergy and drug information, or insurance info you need in an emergency.

❯ The ECG Guide

Developer: QxMD Medical Software
Genre: Medical ✚ **Price:** $4.99
Release: May 17, 2009

Use The ECG Guide as a quick reference with over 175 high-resolution ECG samples. A must for medical professionals and students alike, it covers what you need to know in a simple interface.

❯ Blood Vessel Anatomy

Developer: Simpaddico, LLC ✚ **Genre:** Medical
Price: $0.99 ✚ **Release:** June 13, 2009

Using this handy App you can learn all about the human body's circulatory system. Featuring over 100 blood vessels in its main deck, Blood Vessel Anatomy is ideal for medical and biology students.

❯ Speed Brain

Developer: Lumosity ✚ **Genre:** Medical
Price: $0.99 ✚ **Release:** April 19, 2009

Train your brain to process information faster with Speed Brain. It provides a mental workout that will help you read and react to information, and even allows you to compare your results against others who have tried it.

EyeChart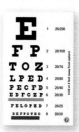

Developer: Dok, LLC **+ Genre:** Medical
Price: FREE **+ Release:** October 7, 2008

Looking for a quick and easy way to measure your visual acuity? Try out this pocket sized version of the famous Snellen eye chart. Place it in front of you and see how well you see!

Dog First Aid

Developer: PetMD **+ Genre:** Medical
Price: $1.99 **+ Release:** June 15, 2009

Confused about what to do with your dog in a medical emergency? Is he overheated or does he need CPR? Tap into Dog First Aid for the answers to your canine medical questions.

BLACKBAG

Developer: Ortho-McNeil-Janssen Pharmaceuticals, Inc
Genre: Medical **+ Price:** FREE
Release: June 2, 2009

Offering news, resources and tools in the world of healthcare, BLACKBAG is a must-have for anyone in the medical profession. With breaking news, videos and access to podcasts, BLACKBAG's coverage is surprisingly deep.

uHear

Developer: Unitron Hearing Limited **+ Genre:** Medical
Price: FREE **+ Release:** April 24, 2009

Think that hearing loss only affects older people? Not so. Hearing loss can begin at any age. Test your hearing acuity with uHear and listen in on some tips for keeping your ears healthy.

Medical

Pocket Guitar

Developer: Shinya Kasatani ✦ **Genre:** Music
Price: $0.99 ✦ **Release:** December 17, 2008

❯ Summary

Toss that vintage 1980s flying-V air guitar you love playing into the closet and step up to Pocket Guitar for your iPhone or iPod Touch. This is no guitar game: you have to press down on the frets, strum, and pluck strings just like the real thing. Featuring six different guitars including acoustic-electric, electric, classical and muted guitars as well as an upright bass and ukulele, this is nirvana for string strummers. There are also a ton of tweaks to choose from, including distortion and wah-wah effects.

❯ Why we like it

This title is a cool demonstration of the iPhone and iPod Touch's remarkable functionality, but it took a few versions to really dial it in. The developers have clearly worked hard to make sure their product remains the best guitar simulator available. Playing Pocket Guitar is as close to the real thing as it gets in Apps instrument simulators, and there's nothing like plucking the strings to get that sweet sound you crave. If you already play or just have an interest in learning more about guitars, Pocket Guitar is worth a try.

[Confused by the seemingly unreadable menu screens? Go to options and change the language from Japanese to English. This App was made in Japan so that is the standard language. German is also available, and more languages are coming soon.]

quick review
★★★☆☆

SIRIUS XM Premium Online

Developer: SIRIUS XM Radio, Inc. + **Genre:** Music
Price: FREE + **Release:** June 3, 2009

Summary

Love your Sirius or XM radio but can never get enough? Have satellite radio in your car and want to take it with you everywhere you go? Then SIRIUS XM Premium Online is the App for you. If you're already a Premium subscriber, this App is not only free to download, it's free to use. Not a subscriber yet? Sirius and XM make it easy to listen to hundreds of commercial free radio stations, the best talk and news, and sports around the clock including the NFL, NBA, NHL and Major League Baseball.

Why we like it

SIRIUS XM Premium Online has a really cool user interface. Some of the actual radios branded by the companies don't look this good. Of course, this App is all about sounds, not sights, and everything you love about your satellite radio is here. Every channel (with the exception of Howard Stern) is included, and you'll always have great sound wherever you are thanks to your device's connections. If you like a song that's being played, be sure to tag it to bookmark or buy it straight away from the iTunes Store, an awesome extra.

[If you look in the App Store, SIRIUS XM Premium Online is not as highly rated as most of the other Apps in this "Best of" book. It has gotten many low reviews for one reason: it lacks the Howard Stern channels. If you're not a Stern fan, you'll love this App.]

Top 100s By Year

Developer: nuTsie + **Genre:** Music
Price: $1.99 + **Release:** June 14, 2009

▶ Summary

Want to hear the biggest hits from the days of your youth all the way up to 2008? Then check out nuTsie's Top 100s By Year, a collection of the biggest hit songs from 1950 to today. See what songs have stood the test of time and rediscover old favorites. The lists aren't based on the Billboard results from that year, nor are they based on total album sales (nuTsie says there'd be too much Michael Bolton to do that). Instead, the songs are carefully selected based on their lasting impact on the world of music.

▶ Why we like it

This is an incredibly cool App for lovers of music history and pop culture. It's great to see the evolution of music over six decades. The songs are arranged in a shuffle based on the year selected, which may irk some who are looking for specific tunes but is generally a cool feature. The whole idea behind the App is to listen to the biggest songs of that year with no regard to rank or chronological order, and it succeeds admirably. You'll find yourself loving this App, and with thousands of songs available, you'll have hours of listening enjoyment.

If you enjoy nuTsie's music Apps then you might want to check out the Music Mega Pack, a collection of 30 different music Apps that features access to tens of thousands of songs. Remember though, you need a 3G or WiFi connection to properly stream all the tunes.

Iheart radio

eveloper: Clear Channel Broadcasting, Inc. + **Genre:** Music
Price: FREE + **Release:** September 8, 2008

Summary

Love music and love your favorite radio station? Then iheart radio is the App for you. Bringing you tons of free music in a great-looking package, there's a station for everyone on iheart radio. Even though it's a music App, there's plenty of stuff to keep you riveted, including talk, political commentary, special interests, and sports radio. The display is big and bold, showing you artist information and the album cover, and even allows you to access song lyrics or tag a song to go back and buy later.

Why we like it

There are lots of Apps with internet radio stations, but not too many that bring together real music stations that air over regular radio. This App is great for lovers of all kinds of music, and as Clear Channel's stations run the gamut from pop to hip-hop to jazz and even talk, there's something for everyone. It's also nice for when you're away from home and want a taste of your old favorite station— since the stations stream live, you can tune in to one or sometimes several stations from your home market no matter where you are.

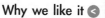

Enjoying iheart radio but looking to try a new station? Don't go digging through all the stations right away: try shaking your iPhone or iPod Touch to tune in to a random station from somewhere across the nation. Who knows, you may find a new favorite channel!

quick review
★★★★☆

Pandora

Developer: Pandora, Inc. + **Genre:** Music
Price: FREE + **Release:** July 9, 2008

> Summary

The best personalized radio playlist application available in the App Store, Pandora allows users to discover and enjoy music from any genre. Simply type in a favorite artist, then sit back and enjoy as Pandora takes you on a spin through similar artists while sprinkling in selections from the artist whose "station" you have created.

> Why we like it

Pandora works as it should every time we tap in. Fast-loading and featuring a simple, clean interface, Pandora sets the standard for a well-designed user interface. Sound quality is also top-notch and more than serviceable for playing in a car over the stereo.

Like the regular web-based Pandora service, Pandora's entry in the App Store is absolutely free. The service used over 400 musical attributes and 2,000 traits to select music, leading to nearly perfect song selection. The service has a painless 30 second registration, and after that it's all music, all the time. Pandora is a premier service that has been continuously tweaked over time, and its iTunes Store link just carries the App one step further.

> Find something you really like? Make sure you bookmark the song in Pandora so you can look it up later. From the profile list on your device or on the web you can view your bookmarked songs and in most cases buy them from online music stores.

quick review
★★★★★

Shazam

Developer: Shazam Entertainment, Ltd. ✦ **Genre:** Music
Price: FREE ✦ **Release:** July 7, 2008

Summary

A unique App when it hit the scene in the summer of 2008, Shazam continues to provide one of the slickest feature sets among Music Apps. With the ability to identify songs playing in your surroundings with the touch of a button, Shazam provides artist and song info, links to purchase songs in the iTunes Store, and links to cool extras like videos on YouTube. It also provides a history of songs that have been tagged, allowing users to go back and look through recently discovered songs.

Why we like it

Shazam is cool, period. Using the musical fingerprint of a song, it can identify the information of over eight million songs—nearly anything users can throw at it. It is the ultimate answer to the age-old question: "what IS that song I hear playing?" Best of all, Shazam is free. That said, the free functionality is starting to come at a price in the form of small ads embedded in the software.

Shazam is available for several other mobile platforms, but the App Store version is by far the most accurate and full-featured edition thanks to the speed and capabilities of your iPhone or iPod Touch.

Apps Capsules

⊘ Adaptunes

Developer: Alpha Acid, LLC ✚ **Genre:** Music
Price: $0.99 ✚ **Release:** June 17, 2009

Want the iPod function of your iPhone or iPod Touch to react smartly when you're in the car? Adaptunes will raise or lower the volume of your music as your vehicle speeds up or slows down.

⊘ Instant Beat—Player

Developer: Instant Binary AB ✚ **Genre:** Music
Price: FREE ✚ **Release:** June 7, 2009

A free drum machine for your iPhone or iPod Touch, Instant Beat puts the power of a full-featured kit in your hands. Try out the full version for six different kits!

⊘ Aura

Developer: Hige Five ✚ **Genre:** Music
Price: $0.99 ✚ **Release:** June 13, 2009

Sit back and relax and listen to the ambient music produced by Aura. It generates sound with four melody instruments and features interactive floating background images that can transport your mind to a relaxed state.

⊘ Sonifi

Developer: Sonik Architects ✚ **Genre:** Music
Price: $4.99 ✚ **Release:** June 16, 2009

Showing off futuristic new music and remixes, Sonifi is a portable remix engine. Link up with a friend and remix tunes together over four channels and four unique tracks, offering unmatched flexibility.

Public Radio Tuner

Developer: American Public Media **+ Genre:** Music
Price: FREE **+ Release:** January 30, 2009

Wish you could hear your favorite public radio
station from home, or just looking to catch a new
spin on the topics you enjoy? Public Radio Tuner
has access to streams of public radio from all
around the country.

Amazing Slow Downer Lite

Developer: Roni Music **+ Genre:** Music
Price: FREE **+ Release:** March 27, 2009

Do you learn new pieces of music by hearing
them over and over and breaking them down in
your head? Try Amazing Slow Downer, which will
replay clips for you and slow them down for
quicker comprehension.

ArtOnAir Player

Developer: ArtOnAir **+ Genre:** Music
Price: FREE **+ Release:** March 27, 2009

Interested in art and experimental music?
Check out ArtOnAir, an internet radio station
specializing in art talk and cultural music. Listen
to their live stream, podcasts, and dig the archives
with this nifty App.

LyricFind Lite

Developer: Lyric Find **+ Genre:** Music
Price: FREE **+ Release:** April 16, 2009

Looking for perfect lyrics to your favorite songs?
Check out LyricFind, which catalogs songs from over
2,000 publishers. Bookmark your favorite lyrics or
click on an artist to find out more about them!

MapQuest 4 Mobile

Developer: AOL **+ Genre:** Navigation
Price: FREE **+ Release:** June 9, 2009

> Summary

One of the original mapping websites, MapQuest has had to reinvent itself several times to stay ahead of the curve. It still offers the detailed and effective turn-by-turn directions that users remember from the website, but there's much more in this App. The MapQuest team has redesigned the function of the App for the iPhone, bringing fantastic tap controls to the maps. Find hotels, restaurants and gas stations with ease and best of all, continue to follow the great maps that have made MapQuest a trusted name in navigation.

> Why we like it

Even though your iPhone has its Maps App, MapQuest 4 Mobile is still worth a look for a number of reasons: The "Find Me" function is always nice to have; if you're lost, you can quickly zoom in on yourself to see what's around you. From there, you can designate a route and follow it in either list form or on the map itself, giving you flexibility. You can also save your most-often used routes, and each trip allows for multiple stops, meaning you don't have to enter or re-enter each as you go.

[Confused about which way to head when a direction tells you to turn in a compass direction? MapQuest 4 Mobile includes arrows on each turn, telling you exactly which way to go.]

quick review
★★★★★

MotionX GPS

Developer: MotionX + **Genre:** Navigation
Price: $2.99 + **Release:** May 28, 2009

Summary

MotionX GPS is one of the bestselling navigation Apps out there and with its powerful list of features, it's easy to see why. With over one million downloads, it's the preferred choice of mountain bikers, hikers, skiers, runners, and sailors. Making use of the iPhone 3G's GPS capabilities, MotionX GPS allows you to view your position at any time on a road or topographical map. MotionX GPS can follow your route back to where you started; track statistics about your trip including time elapsed, distance covered and average speed; and always plots your location accurately with the built-in compass and coordinates.

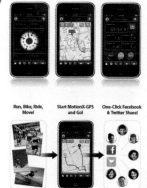

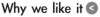

Run, Bike, Ride, Move! — Start MotionX-GPS and Go! — One-Click Facebook & Twitter Share!

Why we like it

This is one powerful App! Need to let friends know where you are? You can e-mail them your complete trip details, including your current location and a picture of yourself wherever you are. If you're on the go, you can save up to 303 different waypoints for your journey. Once you have a waypoint saved, you can view the track you're taking to it and even see your estimated time of arrival based on your current speed.

[Although MotionX GPS can run on the first generation iPhone and iPod Touch, MotionX recommends that you only use the App on the iPhone 3G. The upgraded GPS capabilities are better equipped to handle the rigors of providing constantly updated and precise coordinates.]

quick review
★★★★☆

Geocaching

Developer: Groundspeak, Inc. **+ Genre:** Navigation
Price: $9.99 **+ Release:** January 2, 2009

> Summary

Unfamiliar with geocaching? It's a real-life, real-time global treasure hunt where players locate hidden containers, or geocaches, outdoors and then share their experiences with friends online. With over 700,000 geocaches in play around the world, it's no wonder that there is now a Geocaching App for sale. Featuring four different languages, Geocaching allows users to connect to geocaching.com's database of locations worldwide. The App downloads information about the different geocaches, including the description of the container, tips for finding it, and information about people who have found it recently.

> Why we like it

The world of GPS hunting for caches is a relatively new phenomenon, but with an emphasis on community and a healthy respect for the environment, it's easy to see why it has caught on with so many people. When you're hunting down "treasure", it's always nice to have a treasure map, and Geocaching is the best utility out there for reaching your goal. With full navigating capabilities, Geocaching also allows users to upload notes about their finds to the web.

Geocaching can be as casual or as serious as you want it to be. Many geocaches are easy to locate and require minimal navigational skills, but offer a great way to get into this eco-friendly hobby.

Park Maps

Developer: Big Air Software, LLC ✦ **Genre:** Navigation
Price: $0.99 ✦ **Release:** March 29, 2009

Summary

Love the great outdoors but wish you had a better way to get around our national parks than by unfolding a cumbersome collection of maps? You need Park Maps, an App that delivers as advertised with over 250 maps of U.S. National Parks, National Monuments, and Recreation Areas. All the big names are here including Yellowstone, Yosemite, Grand Canyon, Sequoia, and the Statue of Liberty. If you like hitting the road in your RV, camping in our nation's most beautiful areas, and going on long hikes, then you need Park Maps.

Why we like it

In addition to the big attractions, there are a multitude of lesser-known park areas for you to navigate through. From Denali in Alaska to Isle Royale in Michigan and all the way down to Canaveral in Florida, there are maps for parks peppered all over the country. This App is great even if you just have a bit of wander-lust—you can spend hours just combing through the parks, dreaming about trips you might someday take.

Navigation

While the App is great for giving you a general idea of where to head in a national park, it's a good idea to combine the maps with another App for more serious trail navigation. Try combining the use of Park Maps with MotionX GPS to get an enhanced hiking experience.

quick review
★★★★☆

ManGo

Developer: Linkworks, LLC + **Genre:** Navigation
Price: FREE + **Release:** April 23, 2009

▶ Summary

Featuring over 300 retail chains, ManGo is the go-to App when it comes to finding an outlet of your favorite restaurants, grocers, apparel stores, or even big box retail outlets. You can browse through the different categories to find the name of the chain you're looking for or type it into the search box, making finding your favorites a snap.

▶ Why we like it

If you're looking for a restaurant finder, the price of ManGo can't be beat, since it's free. It also factors in your location by graying out destinations outside of a certain radius so you don't waste your time looking up an outlet that's far away. The number of chains available to search is big and nationwide—you can look up your favorite sporting goods retailer in another city while searching for a branch of your hometown bank. All the big names are here from Wal-Mart and CVS to the U.S. Post Office and McDonald's.

quick review
★★★☆☆

TrafficInfo

Developer: dedfar + **Genre:** Navigation
Price: FREE + **Release:** November 28, 2008

Summary

Using Yahoo's traffic service as a backbone, TrafficInfo allows users to enter their city or ZIP code to find out what might be causing delays on the roads around them. If you frequently drive in an area, especially an urban center where traffic is always a concern, then TrafficInfo is worth a look. Since it doesn't have a built-in map there's no wait time for loading, and if you want to take a closer look at a trouble spot, just tap on an incident and TrafficInfo will zoom you to the location in Google Maps.

Why we like it

If you drive in or near a big city, this App's usefulness is obvious. City traffic is unpredictable and unexpected traffic delays can be maddening. Using TrafficInfo, it's easy to see the trouble spots and steer clear of problems. Note that the App works best in bigger cities, but naturally, that's where most of the traffic is. If you want to try and save some time and frustration, give the user-friendly TrafficInfo a look.

This App is incredibly useful in the areas it covers, and makes navigating around traffic a little easier. Be forewarned though, not every population center is covered, so make sure you live in an area the App services before downloading.

Apps Capsules

◉ MapsBuddy

Developer: Spice Loop + **Genre:** Navigation
Price: $0.99 + **Release:** January 16, 2009

A perfect companion to your device's built-in Maps App, MapsBuddy helps you find the things you're looking for. To find a coffee shop or any other destination, just tap the button on MapsBuddy to find what's near you.

◉ Adventurer

Developer: Mad Ears + **Genre:** Navigation
Price: $1.99 + **Release:** May 20, 2009

Featuring a database of hundreds of cool destinations and a smoothly integrated compass, Adventurer will point you in the direction of something swell no matter where you are!

◉ Where

Developer: uLocate Communications
Genre: Navigation + **Price:** FREE
Release: October 17, 2008

Looking to connect with the people and places around you? The location-identifying Where helps to make you feel like a native of wherever you are. Helping you find Zipcars, restaurants, even cheap gas, Where can find it all!

◉ BackTrack

Developer: Parametrix Software + **Genre:** Navigation
Price: $0.99 + **Release:** September 9, 2008

Ever get so lost that you just want to find your way back to where you came from? Try out BackTrack, which can save up to three locations and help you find your way back to any of them.

HopStop

Developer: HopStop.com + **Genre:** Navigation
Price: FREE + **Release:** January 22, 2009

Operating similarly to the handy website, HopStop
helps you navigate the public transportation
network, taxi routes, and walking areas of several
major U.S. cities. Look for London and Paris to be
added soon.

FastFood

Developer: Kuchbi, Inc. + **Genre:** Navigation
Price: FREE + **Release:** May 11, 2009

It may not be the healthiest food, but sometimes
you just need a quick bite or want something
greasy and FastFood can help satisfy your
cravings. It can find over 75 chains and features
one-tap dialing of the restaurants.

OneTap Movies

Developer: Avantar, LLC + **Genre:** Navigation
Price: FREE + **Release:** June 16, 2009

Looking to see a movie playing near you? Check
out OneTap Movies, which uses your device's
location awareness to find a theater near your
current spot. See show times, read about the
movies, and even watch trailers.

iWant Pro

Developer: Rudrajit Samanta Software
Genre: Navigation + **Price:** $0.99
Release: April 16, 2009

A combination of movie showtimes, restaurant
reviews, and yellow pages, iWant packs a ton
of power into one App. It can search either your
current location or a manually entered destination
for the places you want to go.

Yahoo!

Developer: Yahoo! **+ Genre:** News
Price: FREE **+ Release:** June 3, 2009

> ## Summary
>
It's about way more than news when you Yahoo! Of course, their news section is awesome: breaking headlines are organized in an easy-to-read and highly navigable layout, and links within the App will have you clicking on new stories and learning about new stuff all the time. Yahoo really shines as a total web portal in bringing together your e-mail, instant messenger, weather and news into a neat and dynamic package. If you haven't given it a look, it's worth a try.

> ## Why we like it
>
With all the competition that has surfaced over the last decade, it would have been easy for Yahoo! to go bust like many of its 1990s counterparts. Instead, the dotcom darling has evolved into a robust internet portal that is highly intuitive—there's something to be said for being around a long time and refining your product based on user feedback. Accessing mail from competitors like Gmail is fast and seamless and their news serving is among the best in the e-business.

> If you like your news to automatically update itself, Yahoo! and Yahoo! News support an RSS reader and RSS feeds. Your favorite topics will automatically populate themselves with the top news in the areas that interest you.

quick review
★★★☆☆

NY Times

Developer: The New York Times Company **+ Genre:** News
Price: FREE **+ Release:** April 17, 2009

Summary

The legendary paper is making a name for itself in the mobile world. As other papers struggle for survival in the digital age, the New York Times is seizing the forefront of 'newspaper' technology, as seen with this App. You can now take All the News That's Fit to Print with you on the road, wherever you go. There's no need to be a print subscriber to the paper either, as all the content is free. You may never look at a newspaper the same way again.

Why we like it

There's a reason why the New York Times is the only city newspaper available nationwide: it has some of the deepest and hardest hitting investigative reporting, top-notch editorial content and an interesting mix of content served fresh every day. The mobile App has everything you know and love about the New York Times in an efficient and easily accessible format. Featuring the latest articles and photos from the day, hour, and now minute in news, the App is updated right along with the actual website. The App is also customizable and you can arrange your favorite categories for easier access.

[Did your synchronization get interrupted as you download that day's stories? No worries. Many of the articles are available for offline reading as soon as they're done downloading. If you want to share your favorite articles wait until you get service back and e-mail them.]

quick review
★★★★☆

News Addict
Developer: Tap Mode + **Genre:** News
Price: $0.99 + **Release:** June 10, 2009

◉ Summary

Looking for news stories from all your favorite sites condensed into one App? Look no further than News Addict. Specially formatted to fit your screen, News Addict provides a claimed 25% size advantage over viewing news in the standard Safari browser. It's an easy way to maximize your news reading experience.

Touch controls are easy to use when navigating the news—just touch the lower left corner to maximize or shrink news stories, and you can even tilt your iPhone or iPod Touch to view the news in landscape view.

◉ Why we like it

News Addict is designed for the iPhone and iPod Touch, so the interface is never clunky and always accessible. Being able to go straight to all your favorite news sites is a huge advantage, and simple taps will return you back to the home screen where you can change your news source. All the big names are here, from the New York Times to Time magazine and even web fave Digg.com. You can even watch video from CNN.com or Fox News.

[
With 23 different news sources, News Addict has no bias (or all biases depending on how you look at it) and does a great job of being an outstanding portal to satisfy your news jones. If you don't like the slant of one source, there's sure to be another one that suits you.
]

quick review
★★★☆☆

AP Mobile

Developer: The Associated Press + **Genre:** News
Price: FREE + **Release:** May 18, 2009

Summary

Want to keep up to date with all the latest news, either from across town or around the world? Get all the news as it breaks with AP Mobile from the Associated Press, the world's number one news wire service. With stories about politics, war, entertainment, sports and other topics, AP Mobile covers everything you want to know. With photo galleries and videos updated as soon as they are available, AP Mobile might just be the definitive news feed you've been looking for.

Why we like it

If you want the news, why not go straight to the place where newspapers get much of their content? For pure scope of information, there's nothing better than the Associated Press. For the considerable volume of news the organization generates, AP Mobile is easy to navigate and use. Stories fit into logical categories, and switching from local to national to international stories is a snap. And to help news junkies avoid reading the same thing twice, AP Mobile grays out stories you've already opened.

[AP Mobile allows you to save your favorite stories to Evernote so you can carry them with you wherever you go. The App's push technology also lets you access the news when the App is closed, sending important news alerts right to your screen.]

quick review
★★★☆☆

The Wall Street Journal

Developer: Dow Jones & Company, Inc. + **Genre:** News
Price: FREE + **Release:** April 15, 2009

> Summary

Need to know the latest information from the financial sector, including market news, trends, financial events and happenings, but don't have the time to run out and pick up that day's WSJ? Now you can carry the number one all-business paper with you no matter where you go. Listen to podcasts and save and share all your favorite Journal stories with just a few taps. With a slick interface, fast load times and all the latest news updated in real-time, you may not need to pick up a physical version of the paper ever again.

> Why we like it

The Wall Street Journal is the financial world's number one source for news on the world and how it affects business, and it's a favorite of readers from elite economists to hard working business people around the globe. The execution of their mobile App has the modern reader-on-the-go in mind, so the buttons are large and the stories are easy to open and read. Beyond the essential news stories, this App also features easily navigable links to exclusive videos and podcasts.

[Want to quickly save your favorite stories to come back and read later in the day? Look in the upper right corner of the screen for the save button to bookmark stories. You can also e-mail your favorite stories to friends and colleagues even if they don't have the App.]

quick review
★★★★☆

Stitcher Radio

Developer: Stitcher, Inc. **+ Genre:** News
Price: FREE **+ Release:** August 15, 2008

Summary ‹

Stitching together your favorite news, sports, entertainment and talk, Stitcher Radio brings together everything you love into on-demand stations, organized into categories. You can listen to any content you feel like accessing, bookmarking your favorite shows to come back to later and listening to any of your content whenever you want or discovering new shows. You can share your favorite content with your friends via e-mail, Facebook and Twitter. Stitcher Radio is constantly evolving, so be sure to pay attention for updates.

Why we like it ‹

This one has won its awards with good reason. You can skip syncing your podcasts manually, you don't need to watch TV, and you don't even need a print newspaper when you've got Stitcher Radio. It covers it all, including many favorites such as NPR, Fox News, CNBC and Bloomberg News. Sports is well covered with national news from ESPN Countdown and the popular Mike & Mike show. There's tech news from IGN and TechCrunch, and don't forget Spanish, French, and Japanese language content for a truly global perspective.

News

The Stitcher Radio developers are aware their App may not be everyone's only source for news and radio programming, so they've made it very easy to share content from it with friends who don't have it.

Apps Capsules

❯ BBCReader

Developer: newwaytoseenews ✛ **Genre:** News
Price: FREE ✛ **Release:** February 28, 2009

Some of the highest-quality news in the world, the BBC is brought to the palm of your hand with BBCReader. Browse worldwide news under many different categories and e-mail your favorites to friends and family.

❯ Newspapers

Developer: David Earnest ✛ **Genre:** News
Price: FREE ✛ **Release:** May 21, 2009

Browse through over 2,000 local and regional newspapers from all 50 states with Newspapers. You can read headlines, view and zoom in on stories, open the full stories in Safari, and e-mail your favorites.

❯ All Things Digital

Developer: All Things Digital ✛ **Genre:** News
Price: FREE ✛ **Release:** May 15, 2009

Devoted to tech news and information for the digital age, All Things Digital has offered breaking news and reviews around the clock on your device since 2007. The App features daily columns, interviews, videos and photos.

❯ AMBER Alert

Developer: Jonathan Zdziarski ✛ **Genre:** News
Price: FREE ✛ **Release:** March 5, 2009

Brought to you by the National Center for Missing & Exploited Children, AMBER Alert is designed to help find children who have gone missing. The App features real-time updates with identification information about the child and abductor.

Television

Developer: Makayama.com + **Genre:** News
Price: $2.99 + **Release:** December 15, 2008

Featuring 85 different shows on 42 worldwide stations, Television brings you the best content from the U.S. and Europe. It's one of the easiest ways to watch TV on your device.

HuffingtonPost.com

Developer: HuffingtonPost.com + **Genre:** News
Price: FREE + **Release:** February 26, 2009

Stay informed in real time with the Huffington Post's mobile App. The App brings you all the great content you've come to expect from the website including streaming video and blog posts.

Rachel Maddow

Developer: The Zumobi Network + **Genre:** News
Price: FREE + **Release:** May 15, 2009

Delivering a smart look at politics and news of the world, Rachel Maddow has become one of the most popular voices in news. Carry her with you wherever you go and have access to watching all her latest segments.

ConsumerReports.org

Developer: Consumer Reports + **Genre:** News
Price: FREE + **Release:** February 25, 2009

Providing mobile news and video on the world of consumer goods, ConsumerReports.org is one of the most trusted voices by you, the consumer. Make sure you're getting the most value in whatever consumer goods you purchase by reading their expert reviews.

News

quick review
★★★☆☆

ColorSplash

Developer: Hendrik Kueck + **Genre:** Photography
Price: $1.99 + **Release:** June 16, 2009

> Summary

Wish you could take better pictures with your iPhone? Give your photos a professional feel by selectively adding and deleting color using ColorSplash. The idea is called "cutout" and it adds drama to any image by juxtaposing the black and white portion of the picture with the color portion, making for some cool photos. With four different brushes and a unique way of changing brush sizes, it offers total control over what has color and what doesn't. It's slick, cool, and easy to use—you'll be making pictures like a pro in no time.

> Why we like it

Hendrik Kueck makes some great photography Apps, including Juxtaposer and other Apps featured in this book. ColorSplash is no exception. With multiple user-friendly features and great functionality, it's easy for anyone looking to improve the state of their photos. One of the most handy features is the ability to work in either portrait or landscape mode, great for getting a better angle on the picture you're editing. If you mess up, ColorSplash has unlimited undos. When you're done manipulating images, you can automatically send them to your Facebook or Twitter account.

[Like ColorSplash but wish you could change the brush size? Here's a nifty solution: zoom in and out by pinching instead. It quickly becomes intuitive and allows for precise control of the brush and section of image you're working on.]

quick review
★★★☆☆

Vihgo

Developer: Vizros Software Mobile + **Genre:** Photography
Price: $1.99 + **Release:** June 18, 2009

Summary ⊘

Want to add cool effects to your pictures without having to upload them to a computer and use expensive photo manipulation software? If you need a simple and quick solution that will help you create studio-caliber pictures, check out Vihgo. With 24 fully-editable filters, Vihgo offers enough variety that you may never need to run your photos through other software again. Featuring popular effects like Old School, Fog, and X-Ray, there's not much missing. Each filter also includes a full set of sliders to really tweak your photos however you wish.

Why we like it ⊘

Not everyone is a photo manipulation expert, and finding the right balance to create a decent-looking photo effect can be daunting. With 24 filters available with Vihgo, finding the right filter is a snap with the Traverse feature. When you activate Traverse, Vihgo responds by slowly working its way through all 24 filters, one at a time. Once you find a filter you like, simply tap your screen to stop the filter rotation and enjoy your new and improved picture!

[
Vihgo's filters also include 3D simulation effects like Page Curl, and every effect allows you to apply it selectively, giving you further freedom over your images. If you like Page Curl, be sure to follow the developers' blog, as they're always adding new filters and effects.
]

quick review
★★★★☆

Camerabag

Developer: Nevercenter Ltd. Co. + **Genre:** Photography
Price: $1.99 + **Release:** May 30, 2009

> Summary

Check out the ten amazing cameras of Camerabag. If you want to make your photos look like those from a bygone era, or to recreate grainy moments from your childhood, check out the emulation layers brought to you in this App. If you don't want to change a thing, try "Original" and you have a great camera App that allows you to save, rename and e-mail photos.

> Why we like it

The functionality of Camerabag is astounding. Not having to switch to another App to change looks is a handy time-saver. No other App changes the appearance of your photos the way Camerabag does—this is truly a unique App. Camerabag even allows you to swap the filters back and forth on a picture you just took. Being able to do this right away saves time on adding filters later and your instant results can be dazzling.

[Want to get deeper looking effects with Camerabag's filters? Try saving a picture, then reload it and apply a different camera style. For example, layering "Instant" with "1974" adds a sweet oldschool photo album look to your pictures.]

quick review
★★★☆☆

Pano

Developer: Debacle Software ✦ **Genre:** Photography
Price: $2.99 ✦ **Release:** June 19, 2009

Summary

Faced with an impressive scene in front of you, but not sure if your iPhone camera can do it justice? Try taking a panoramic shot of the mountains around you or the beach in front of you with Pano. Automatically stitching up to 16 photos together, Pano allows users to take top-quality panoramas without having to use complicated software. With high resolution, built-in tips and easy controls, Pano is a cool photography App.

Why we like it

The interface of Pano is incredibly intuitive, meaning that panoramas have never been easier to make. The stitching looks good, and photos are saved right alongside your others, saving you time so you don't have to dig for your shots. To work, Pano provides semi-transparent grid guides you while you line up your photos, meaning you don't have to guess and potentially leave gaps in your image. Since taking panoramas takes time, Pano will auto-save your progress if you get a text or phone call.

[Want to get some tips on improving the way yours turn out? Take them over to Pano's Flickr page, where you can post your images, check out the work of others, and get tips and comments about how to make your photos look even better.]

quick review
★★★☆☆

PhotoNote

Developer: Bananas Design + **Genre:** Photography
Price: $1.99 + **Release:** June 17, 2009

> Summary

Trying to find that perfect gift you saw in another store? Trying to remember the price of an item to check online and want to make sure you're looking at the same thing? There's a thousand uses for PhotoNote, an incredibly handy App that will leave you wondering how you ever got by without it. It's simple and easy to use—just take a photo and add a note to it, categorizing it so you remember exactly what you want about the image. If you don't want to, or can't, take a picture that's okay too, as the App is also a full-featured notepad.

> Why we like it

How many times have you made a note to yourself only to forget the context? PhotoNote helps to eliminate these frustrations by adding a new dimension to the note-taking process. Not only does it take a photo of the subject of your note, it helps your brain to create a mental image of what you need to remember. You can use PhotoNote to act as a personal memo service or you can be a bit light-hearted and use it as a photo diary, such as cataloging the events of a day sightseeing.

[PhotoNote allows you the option of saving the photos you take in the App to your Picture Library, meaning you don't have to take the picture twice or lose the image forever when you delete a note.]

quick review
★★★☆☆

Photobucket

Developer: Photobucket.com + **Genre:** Photography
Price: FREE + **Release:** April 28, 2009

Summary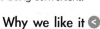

Do you use Photobucket to share your photographs with friends and family online? Wish there was a way to use the most common features of the service to stay connected with Photobucket wherever you go? Check out the mobile App—it's speedy, easy for anyone to use, and is a breeze to upload or browse through your photos. Featuring settings for automatic uploading, easy linking to Facebook, MySpace and other social media outlets, Photobucket is user-friendly in addition to being convenient.

Why we like it

Photobucket's App may not be jam-packed with features, but those that are included are lightning quick and easy, making this a must-download for users of the web service. You can also access Photobucket's main website from a button on the front page of the App, allowing you to go in and perform functions that aren't yet available in the App.

Apps Capsules

> Photo Rotate

Developer: Andrew Bednarz ✛ **Genre:** Photography
Price: $0.99 ✛ **Release:** June 17, 2009

Ever accidentally take a photo with the wrong orientation, or zoomed-out too far? Fix it straight from your device with Photo Rotate. It is a powerful little App that allows you to rotate a photo and crop it.

> PS Tips+

Developer: simpaddico, LLC ✛ **Genre:** Photography
Price: $1.99 ✛ **Release:** June 17, 2009

Tired of navigating all the menus of the powerful Photoshop program? Fire up PS Tips+ and have the full library of shortcuts right at your fingertips. Also features Search if you know what you want but can't find it.

> My New Smile

Developer: RightSprite ✛ **Genre:** Photography
Price: FREE ✛ **Release:** December 31, 2008

Tired of your smile and want to brighten it? Want to add a goofy smile to a picture of friends? Do both with My New Smile and change the way you look in two simple steps.

> Juxtaposer Lite

Developer: Hendrik Kueck ✛ **Genre:** Photography
Price: FREE ✛ **Release:** May 17, 2009

Easily combine any two images in fun and creative ways with Juxtaposer Lite. Erase part of one image and stack it on to a second image to create wacky pictures; it's simple and fun!

Nature

Developer: Juicy Bits ✦ **Genre:** Photography
Price: $0.99 ✦ **Release:** June 16, 2009

Add the cool serenity and stunning beauty of
top-shelf nature photographs to your device with
Nature. Featuring the best images from some of
the most downloaded photographers in the world,
each picture is optimized for your screen.

Pixel Perfect

Developer: Code Monkeys At Work
Genre: Photography ✦ **Price:** FREE
Release: June 16, 2009

Improve your photographs or make fantastic
wallpapers with Pixel Perfect. Add effects like
brightness controls and color filters to your photos
and even share them online using Facebook.

Passport Photo Machine

Developer: James Graeber ✦ **Genre:** Photography
Price: $0.99 ✦ **Release:** June 7, 2009

Now here's an App that pays for itself the first time
you use it! Take passport photos and upload them
to your favorite photo service like Kodak or
Photobucket to print them for processing.

AutoStitch

Developer: Cloudburst Research
Genre: Photography ✦ **Price:** FREE
Release: June 6, 2009

Take panoramic photos to the next level with
AutoStitch, the most comprehensive photo
stitching App in the App Store. Combine multiple
images automatically into a mosaic for stellar
wide-angle shots.

quick review
★ ★ ★ ★ ☆

Bento

Developer: Filemaker, Inc. **+ Genre:** Productivity
Price: $4.99 **+ Release:** June 15, 2009

🔘 Summary

Organize the details of your life all in one place with a terrific interface—Bento. Jam-packed with 25 different database templates that are ready for your information, Bento is a handy home base for your data and organizes it in a thoughtful and highly accessible format. With 15 different fields in each database you can store as much information about a contact, place, or event as you wish. This portable, personal database may soon become one of your favorite Apps.

🔘 Why we like it

Bento is so slick and functional it's almost worthy of being bundled with every new iPhone and iPod Touch sold. If you're an anal, hyper-organized nut job, you'll love Bento. If you're just trying to get all your data in once place, Bento can help you become more efficient at grinding through life. Bento meshes with the rest of an iPhone so well that it feels like a native App. Just tap a Bento contact to make a call, view a website, display a map, or send an e-mail.

[Bento can manage just about every aspect of your life, including guest lists for parties, memberships in a club or fraternity, or even recipes. If you're synchronizing to the desktop application on your Mac, there's no need to hook up to a dock: Bento can handle it all wirelessly.]

quick review
★★★☆☆

Print & Share

Developer: EuroSmartz, Ltd **+ Genre:** Productivity
Price: $6.99 **+ Release:** June 17, 2009

Summary

Want to transfer, view, and print documents from the convenience of wherever-you-are with your iPhone? Look no further than Print & Share, an essential App for people with document needs. A full-featured App that can handle the file formats of just about any office suite, Print & Share brings flexibility to your e-mail, your iPhone and your life. Never again worry about a document format from an attachment—you can handle it and send it on to the next person who needs it. Print & Share also allows you to store many different types of files, so you don't have to immediately forward them on.

Why we like it

This App has so many useful features it's impossible to cover them all. Print & Share has a full web browser built in, so you don't even have to leave the App to find things to print out or visit links sent to you in e-mail. You can print out a list of your contacts in either list or card form, and it can also handle any type of photos, including printing and displaying them from either your iPhone or an e-mail attachment.

[Like what you're seeing on a web page and want to print it out for later? Use Print & Share to print the content of the site over your network printer. If you're not at home, you can even save web pages to print when you get home.]

quick review
★★★☆☆

Grocery Gadget

Developer: Flixoft, Inc. ✦ **Genre:** Productivity
Price: $2.99 ✦ **Release:** June 14, 2009

Summary

Want to become better organized at grocery shopping than just scribbling out a list on a slip of paper before you walk in to the store? Grocery Gadget makes staying organized while shopping easy, fun and cost-effective. Make a list and share it with the whole family so if you're sending out a team of shoppers, they know what to get, and who is getting what. Grocery Gadget also allows you to stay on top of your weekly shopping: you can save lists and use them again.

Why we like it

If you don't want to tap out your entire shopping list on your iPhone or iPod Touch, Grocery Gadget is still the solution for you. Your purchase of the App allows you to use Grocery Gadget's web portal to punch-in your list from a full-sized computer keyboard and later sync to your device, which is especially handy to build your original shopping list. It's a smart App, too. As you tick off items while shopping, Grocery Gadget learns where the items are in the store, helping you to better organize your list the next time you go.

Not sure where you're getting the best deal? Grocery Gadget allows you to enter the price for an item for each store you visit. It makes comparison shopping easier than ever. Also, if you need to send your shopping list to someone, Grocery Gadget allows you to e-mail it.

quick review
★★★★★

Things

Developer: Cultured Code ✦ **Genre:** Productivity
Price: $9.99 ✦ **Release:** June 18, 2009

Summary

It's the number one paid to-do App available, and it's easy to see why. Things helps you get things done as if you had your own personal assistant helping you every step of the way.

Simple, focused, and never cumbersome, Things allows you to enter in plenty of detail and provides enough flexibility and power to make it a fantastic time manager. Be sure to use the Tags system to help you organize even further.

Why we like it

Time management software can suffer from two main ills—it's either too bulky and overweight to be useful, or so simplified and basic that it doesn't help you get things done. Things strikes a balance between them and its file system is simple, intuitive, and fun to use.

The App is always being updated. Another standout feature is the wireless syncing over WiFi for users who have bought the desktop version of Things.

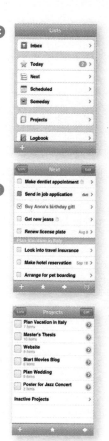

Productivity

> With six different languages and nearly endless possibilities for files and folders, Things can help just about anyone and everyone be more productive. When a bug is found, the developers are quick to respond—bug fixes are usually available within a week.

quick review
★★★★☆

OmniFocus

Developer: The Omni Group + **Genre:** Productivity
Price: $19.99 + **Release:** June 14, 2009

> Summary

Looking for more out of your task management software? Not sure where to look with so many different options out there? Give OmniFocus a look. Packed with features you'll find in no other run-of-the-mill task manager, OmniFocus has the tools you need to get 'er done. It can organize your tasks based on your location and what's nearest you, and even allows you to record voice notes about the tasks you need to do, or just completed.

> Why we like it

Have an errand to run? Mark down the place you need to go to and OmniFocus will integrate with your Maps App to pinpoint your destination. A tap on the balloon on the map will reveal the details of your errand. When you have a bunch of places to go all over town, there's nothing more useful. It will even tell you right away what you need to do at each location, so you're not scratching your head and having to go back to look through your tasks. The App also syncs with the desktop version and MobileMe wirelessly, a required feature for the top-shelf time management Apps.

[The newest version of OmniFocus has added several new features to what was already a fantastic App. For example, using the Repeat screen, you can set up a task to replay at a certain date, such as visiting the dentist a week after a checkup for a follow-up exam.]

mSecure

Developer: mSeven Software, LLC **+ Genre:** Productivity
Price: $2.99 **+ Release:** February 9, 2009

Summary

A secure data manager and password keeper
for your iPhone or iPod Touch, mSecure takes
password management to perhaps its most
secure level. Using industry standard encryption techniques, your data is safe when it's
stored behind mSecure. When you're on the
go, accessing your information is quick and
easy, and if you forget your password, you
can set a hint to try to jog your memory.
Keep your data safe with mSecure!

Why we like it

This is an App that knows what its users are
looking for out of password storage. Simple
and secure, mSecure has an easy interface
that takes only minutes to learn. The App runs
fast and the controls quickly become intuitive,
so you'll be entering data in no time. mSecure
realizes that not all login information is the
same, so it offers 17 different categories to
choose from when entering your data to get
you started quickly. You can also add your
own custom types of entries and icons for
maximum flexibility.

If you buy mSecure for a limited time, mSeven Software is offering the
desktop companion software free of charge. For only $2.99, that's a
lot of value out of an App that provides so much security. In the event
of a crash on either end, you can backup and restore your data so no
passwords are lost in oblivion.

Apps Capsules

◉ EasyWriter

Developer: Saxorama.net ✦ **Genre:** Productivity
Price: FREE ✦ **Release:** April 6, 2009

Take your e-mail writing skills to the next level with EasyWriter. Most notably, it allows you to read and reply in landscape mode, but it also auto-saves your typing when you get a text message or phone call.

◉ Palringo Instant Messenger Lite

Developer: Palringo Limited ✦ **Genre:** Productivity
Price: FREE ✦ **Release:** July 23, 2008

Seamlessly combine your instant messaging networks with Palringo, an elegant and fast App for your IM needs. Send voice and picture messages or create groups across networks to send messages to your friends.

◉ Sleepmaker Storms Free

Developer: Saxorama.net ✦ **Genre:** Productivity
Price: FREE ✦ **Release:** June 12, 2009

Having trouble falling asleep or falling into a deeper sleep? Try Sleepmaker Storms, recorded in high quality from real storms, not sound effects. With options for gentle or hard storms, you'll be snoozing in no time.

◉ YouMail

Developer: YouMail, Inc. ✦ **Genre:** Productivity
Price: FREE ✦ **Release:** March 31, 2009

No access to a desktop to check your YouMail voicemail? No problem with the YouMail App, which brings complete access to the service. You can even record new messages and greetings.

FileAid

Developer: DigiDNA + **Genre:** Productivity
Price: FREE + **Release:** May 27, 2009

Easily copy files from your computer onto your iPhone or iPod Touch with FileAid. Powerful but user-friendly, FileAid's easy-to-use interface will make sure you're never hunting down a file again.

Remember The Milk

Developer: Remember The Milk + **Genre:** Productivity
Price: FREE + **Release:** December 12, 2008

If you already have a Remember The Milk account, then you need to get the App. The award-winning task management service allows you to carry your list of things to do with you anywhere.

AntiStress Painter

Developer: flandolsi + **Genre:** Productivity
Price: FREE + **Release:** April 4, 2009

Paint your feelings onto your iPhone or iPod Touch with the AntiStress Painter. With a set of five brushes and vivid colors you can create patterns that you aren't even consciously aware of.

Productivity

AppSniper

Developer: Manta Research + **Genre:** Productivity
Price: $0.99 + **Release:** March 7, 2009

Spending too much in the App Store or just want to wait for a good deal on the App you've been eyeing? Pay for AppSniper with its first use. This App for Apps monitors the App Store for price changes.

quick review
★★★☆☆

The World Factbook '09

Developer: jDictionary Mobile ✦ **Genre:** Reference
Price: $0.99 ✦ **Release:** June 13, 2009

> ## Summary
Interested in always learning more about the world around you? Need to research someplace for a test or upcoming trip? Check out the App Store's definitive resource on the Planet Earth, The World Factbook '09. With information on more than 250 locations, the Factbook is concise, well-organized and fantastically educational. Plus, The World Factbook isn't just packed with info about countries and territories; it also includes entries on the world's oceans, our changing planet, and areas in dispute like the West Bank and Western Sahara.

> ## Why we like it
The World Factbook has been available on other mobile networks before hitting the App Store, so it's a well-polished and thorough App. It's a must-have application for anyone with an interest in geography or just wanting to know more about places near and far away. The World Factbook is not just a smattering of information: the data within is well-researched and it can be an important source for everyone from students to diplomats. With a fast interface and quick scrolling, this informative App can make anyone feel smarter.

[In all versions, there are hundreds of thousands of users of The World Factbook. It's a snappy reference and once it is downloaded it requires no internet connection. Be sure to bookmark your favorite entries to go back and learn more whenever you wish.]

quick review
★★★★☆

Wiki Mobile

Developer: Comoki Software **+ Genre:** Reference
Price: $1.99 **+ Release:** January 21, 2009

Summary

With hundreds of thousands of articles edited by the internet-going public, Wikipedia is one of the most popular websites and reference tools around. It's a magnificent 21st century resource, and Wiki Mobile seeks to make it mobile with its constantly evolving App. With snappy loading, easily accessible articles and one-touch image opening with the tap function of your iPhone or iPod Touch, Wiki Mobile will have you using Wikipedia in new and far more efficient ways. Featuring both quick and deeper advanced searches, the information you want is always just a few taps away.

Why we like it

It's the power of Wikipedia in a fantastic App that maximizes the full potential of the website. It can display in both portrait and landscape, and is available in 32 different languages. There's a full text search function, an in-App image viewer that displays captions better than the website and features full bookmarking. The formatting of each article fits your screen perfectly, and using Wikipedia has never looked better or been more efficient. If you're a regular Wiki-user, you're going to want this App—it makes the whole Wiki-experience quicker and tidier than ever.

The App is much more accessible than simply visiting Wikipedia in the Safari browser, and there's a lot to keep you using Wiki Mobile. The latest update included the all-important landscape view and a handy back button to track to articles you've already read.

quick review
★★★★☆

Google Mobile App
Developer: Google + **Genre:** Reference
Price: FREE + **Release:** April 28, 2009

> ## Summary
It's the world's most popular search engine. They've created one of the biggest e-mail hubs since e-mail was invented. They're a constantly innovating company with new products and services that are pushing the bounds of technology with each release. Google has proven that they can do it all, and now they've developed the Google Mobile App. It features the powerfully simple search that everyone has become so familiar with, but it also allows users to reach out and visit any of Google's other online offerings.

> ## Why we like it
Perhaps the most fun can be had from speaking your search queries into Google Mobile. The App can handle any English accent, including British and Australian dialects. The results are usually pretty solid, and most of the time you can find what you're looking for without have to type anything in. Being able to access other Google services is also handy. It's nice to be able to navigate right to Google Docs or Google Apps or even to head into Gmail without having to close the application or open another one.

[Looking for search results near you? Google Mobile is location aware, so you don't have to worry about typing in your current area. If you're in New York and type in "pizza", Google will automatically search for a pizza place near you.]

quick review
★★★☆☆

iBird Explorer PRO

Developer: Mitch Waite Group **+ Genre:** Reference
Price: $29.99 **+ Release:** April 25, 2009

Summary

An interactive field guide to nearly 1,000 species of birds native to the United States (including Hawaii), iBird Explorer PRO is the best bird-watching App on any platform. Search for your favorite birds, match them to the App, then take a photo with your device and upload it to Flickr. If you have an interest in birds, then iBird Explorer PRO will help you see our feathered friends in a whole new light.

Why we like it

It's pricey, yes. Still, if you're an avid or beginner bird watcher, iBird Explorer PRO is a must-have App. There are so many functions crammed into it that you'll never want to go birding without it again. The newest version has a date-based search feature, so you can match the birds you see to the month you observed them, giving you a timeline of what you've seen. The other search functions are advanced and detailed: you can search by song, conservation status, species, and banding, meaning there's always some way to find what you're looking for. The large portrait images help you confirm your sightings.

U.S. Historical Documents

Developer: Standard Works, LLC ✦ **Genre:** Reference
Price: $0.99 ✦ **Release:** May 8, 2009

▶ Summary

See how our country was shaped by the men who put the words to paper with U.S. Historical Documents. Featuring over 150 of the documents that helped form the foundation of what America is today, this App covers it all. Starting with the Magna Carta through colonial documents including the Mayflower Compact and First Thanksgiving Proclamation, the App has the earliest days of America covered. In the revolutionary 1700s there's the infamous Stamp Act followed by the famous Declaration of Independence. From the Constitution all the way up to President Obama's 2009 speech to the joint session of Congress, if it's an important document in American history, it's here.

▶ Why we like it

It's hard to find this many significant documents in one resource, whether in an App or anywhere else. It's a must-have App for any student of United States history or any person with an interest in democracy. The user-friendly functions are a welcome addition: you can search for and bookmark documents, annotate within the documents, and even highlight important passages to come back to later.

There are plenty of fun and light hearted Apps in the App Store, but as far as serious reference goes, it's hard to beat U.S. Historical Documents. The makers of the App truly listen to their users, as the latest version added over 40 documents by user request. Props to them!

quick review
★★★☆☆

Advanced Dictionary and Thesaurus

Developer: jDictionary Mobile **+ Genre:** Reference
Price: $0.99 **+ Release:** May 26, 2009

Summary

The premier mobile dictionary and thesaurus is now available on your iPhone and iPod Touch. Ready to go at a moment's notice, Advanced Dictionary and Thesaurus will find just the word you're looking for and tell you more about it than you could have ever hoped to look up in books. Because the App displays so much information about the word you looked up (famous examples, roots, and all related words), you're sure to learn something about anything you type in. You might even start using the App for trivial fun!

Why we like it

The Advanced Dictionary and Thesaurus is no shallow App. It's on several other mobile platforms and has become a trusted source for students, writers and speakers of the English language. Few Apps combine the dictionary and thesaurus elements so well, and no other App has the extras that Advanced Dictionary and Thesaurus has. A slick interface and dynamite controls help make this a fantastic reference App.

Advanced Dictionary and Thesaurus has many more words than your average physical reference book. With over 250,000 entries, the App covers over 1.5 million words. There are countless matches, synonyms and antonyms to look up and learn.

Apps Capsules

❯ Xbox Achievement Guide

Developer: UIEvolution, Inc. ✦ **Genre:** Reference
Price: FREE ✦ **Release:** February 23, 2009

Stuck trying to get to 100% completion on your favorite games? Hold a handy pocket reference right next to you with the Xbox Achievement Guide. Increase your gamer points, find hidden achievements, and get more out of your games.

❯ iThesaurus

Developer: Desire Life Software ✦ **Genre:** Reference
Price: FREE ✦ **Release:** February 23, 2009

Stuck on a crossword puzzle or just need to know some synonyms or antonyms? Fire up iThesaurus for a database of 140,000 words that will help expand your vocabulary. It also includes definitions.

❯ Math Ref Free

Developer: Happy Maau Studios ✦ **Genre:** Reference
Price: FREE ✦ **Release:** April 16, 2009

The free version of the incredibly useful Math Ref, Math Ref Free is a powerful App on its own. It's packed with formulas, tips and tricks for algebra, geometry, trigonometry and even calculus.

❯ 25,000 Baby Names

Developer: DMBC ✦ **Genre:** Reference
Price: FREE ✦ **Release:** March 2, 2009

With a database of names spanning over two dozen different origins, 25,000 Baby Names has the name you're looking for. Search through both boys, and girls, names and go deeper by learning the meaning behind each name.

Area Codes <

Developer: VersaEdge Software + **Genre:** Reference
Price: $0.99 + **Release:** May 26, 2009

Ever get a phone call from an area code you don't recognize? Fire up Area Codes and type in the three digits to find out exactly where your call came from or search by city.

Yahoo! Answers <

Developer: Western ITS Limited + **Genre:** Reference
Price: FREE + **Release:** August 19, 2008

With over 100 million answered questions, Yahoo! Answers is a prime example of a successful community-driven website. Take the power of the database on the road with you or post a question for other users to answer.

VocabDaily Free <

Developer: Taptation + **Genre:** Reference
Price: FREE + **Release:** October 25, 2008

Expand your vocabulary knowledge through Merriam-Webster Words of the Day. View all the information about the words including origin and definition in the App's tabbed interface, and even bookmark your favorites.

FREE Grammar Up <

Developer: Eknath Kadam + **Genre:** Reference
Price: FREE + **Release:** June 16, 2009

Test your knowledge of English grammar with this fun and intuitive quiz game. Study different and wide-ranging topics of the English language. This App is perfect for both younger students and people learning English as a second language.

Reference

quick review
★★★★☆

Tweetie

Developer: atebits, Inc. ✦ **Genre:** Social Networking
Price: $2.99 ✦ **Release:** November 11, 2008

❯ Summary

It's not just another Twitter App—Tweetie
is a fully-featured and incredibly powerful
App that will put a whole new spin on your
Tweetin'. With features that make the official
website seem almost anemic, Tweetie is well
worth the purchase price. Reply to threads
inline, browse the web from within the App,
and browse all your friends and followers
with ease. You can set your location, upload
pictures to TwitPic and even link to StockTwits
with Tweetie. Basically, if it's doable on
Twitter, you can do it quickly, painlessly,
and with ease using Tweetie!

❯ Why we like it

If you Tweet on the go, then you must have
Tweetie! It's a top-notch Tweeting application
for a number of reasons: it's stylish, incredibly
fast, has an attractive user interface and,
above all, is incredibly easy to use. It can
handle multiple Twitter accounts and works
well with your favorites, making operation
seamless. Technically, Tweetie transmits
your data over a secure connection, and
even features landscape typing—a major
bonus for people who don't want to always
type in portrait view. Automatic link sharing
and posting are other nice pluses.

[There are several Apps out there for updating Twitter, but none are as
feature-rich as Tweetie. What makes it tick best is speed—Tweetie is
blazingly fast. It loads quickly, scrolling is powerful and remarkably
quick, and updates are posted in seemingly instantaneous fashion.]

quick review
★★★★☆

WhosHere

Developer: myRete **+ Genre:** Social Networking
Price: FREE **+ Release:** May 29, 2009

Summary

A fantastic new program for meeting new and like-minded people, WhosHere helps you find others for dating, friendships, work networking, or even just text chatting. Fill out your profile and WhosHere will instantly show you a list of people that match your interests in your area. If you're mobile, you can open up WhosHere to spot matches that are close to you and feel free to send messages to your new matches. With no fees for the App and no SMS fees, WhosHere is worth a knock-knock!

Why we like it

Because WhosHere now has over 400,000 users, there's always someone nearby. The anonymity is a plus—you can exchange messages with someone without ever giving out your phone number, e-mail address or IM screen name. Of course, if you want to get personal and even meet in person, WhosHere allows you to make the introduction. The ability to use the program when you briefly lose service is a plus as well, since you can still read your unread messages and compose replies that'll be sent as soon as you get signal back.

Social Networking

WhosHere doesn't just help you to meet new people; you may even reconnect with old friends as well. Also, WhosHere may discover an interest you have with a friend that you may not have known about before.

quick review
★★★★☆

fring

Developer: fringland, Ltd. **+ Genre:** Social Networking
Price: FREE **+ Release:** October 1, 2008

Summary

A mobile community communication service that allows users over many popular networks to connect, fring maximizes the potential of many different services, including Skype, AIM, Yahoo Messenger and Twitter. You can stay connected at all times with your friends from all the networks, conveniently displayed together on your screen. Share experiences and never lose touch with the ones you love thanks to the ability to both instant message and talk to them using VoIP technology and your iPhone or iPod Touch's WiFi connection.

Why we like it

While there are plenty of Apps that allow your messaging lists from different services to come together under one banner, no one does it with better style and substance than fring. The ability to not only instant message but to connect over VoIP is a fantastic feature that makes communicating with friends a snap. Your contact list is always dynamic as long as you're connected, meaning you have the most up-to-date information about your friends' statuses. Because nearly every major network is supported, you don't have to worry about losing track of a contact.

[fring allows users the unique ability to stay connected to the network even when the application is closed. Though the feature doesn't cover all the continents yet, it works in the United States. The App gets better with every update and is worth a try since it's free!]

quick review
★★★☆☆

iWallFlower

Developer: iCloseBy.com ✦ **Genre:** Social Networking
Price: `FREE` ✦ **Release:** February 19, 2009

Summary

Automatically share your doodles and drawings with friends or strangers all over the world with iWallFlower. An "emotional networking" App, iWallFlower can be appreciated by anyone who can understand the universal language spoken by art. Turn on the App and you're greeted by scrolling images drawn by other users of the App from around the world. You can see their emotions and feelings go by you in real time, and you can vote for the ones you like. The more votes a drawing gets, the more it will be displayed.

Why we like it

iWallFlower is as simple to use as you want it to be. If you can draw a stick figure, you posses the ability to use the App to contribute your own art. The brushes are simple but at the same time there is surprising depth to the App, with many options for the brushes and colors, making each piece unique. Best of all, if you're not an artist you can still appreciate iWallFlower as you don't need to generate any content to use the App. Simply sit back and enjoy the original images of art that unfold before you.

[You can see and compare your drawings with other users around the world, but iWallFlower lets you get in on the local art scene by allowing you to just view drawings posted by users in your area, or elsewhere around the world.]

Apps Capsules

❯ Omeagle

Developer: Leif K-Brooks
Genre: Social Networking
Price: $0.99 ✦ **Release:** May 28, 2009

A fun way to meet new people, Omeagle can be as anonymous as you want to be. Fire up the App and you're instantly placed in a random conversation with another Omeagle users.

❯ Bump

Developer: Bump Technologies, LLC
Genre: Social Networking ✦ **Price:** FREE
Release: March 27, 2009

A revolutionary way to exchange your personal information with other iPhones and iPod Touches, Bump allows users to add new contacts simply by bumping devices with each other. No typing, no mistakes, just Bump and go!

❯ Facebook

Developer: Facebook ✦ **Genre:** Social Networking
Price: FREE ✦ **Release:** July 10, 2008

The new, best way to stay in contact with all your friends, the Facebook App makes Facebooking on the go easy. Start chats, post photos and updates, browse your friends and do more with Facebook.

❯ Dating DNA

Developer: Dating DNA, Inc. ✦ **Genre:** Social Networkir
Price: FREE ✦ **Release:** May 1, 2009

One of the most popular dating Apps, Dating DNA is a free way to meet other singles. With compatibility matching and use of GPS to find singles near you, Dating DNA is worth a look for anyone interested.

AIM

Developer: AOL + **Genre:** Social Networking
Price: $2.99 + **Release:** February 26, 2009

Still the king of the hill in instant messaging, AIM lets
you stay connected with all of your contacts and
manage your Buddy List. AIM allows you to connect
using multiple screen names and is easy to use.

Brightkite

Developer: Brightkite.com + **Genre:** Social Networking
Price: FREE + **Release:** October 19, 2008

Want to meet people at the places you frequent?
Try out Brightkite, where you can browse the profiles of people around you, see what your friends
are up to, and even post photos and notes.

Big Canvas PhotoShare

Developer: BigCanvas, Inc. + **Genre:** Social Networking
Price: FREE + **Release:** July 7, 2008

Want to capture your life as it happens and share it
with loved ones? Check out PhotoShare, a new
App for posting the goings on in your life. Just snap
a picture, add a description, and start a-postin'.

Loopt

Developer: Loopt, Inc. + **Genre:** Social Networking
Price: FREE + **Release:** July 4, 2008

Link to the world around you using Loopt, connect-
ing on the fly to share your information with all your
social networks. Update your blogs, Facebook, and
Twitter on the fly—all at the same time if you want.

Social Networking

quick review
★★★★☆

MLB.com At Bat 2009

Developer: Major League Baseball Advanced Media
Genre: Sports ✦ **Price:** $9.99 ✦ **Release:** March 29, 2009

❯ Summary

Utilizing the technology found in their web-based Gameday service, MLB.com At Bat is a fantastic way to follow your favorite team. It's as close as you can get to a game without a ticket or television, and tracking the game is a snap thanks to the Gameday graphics. With full box score information and updating video highlights as the game goes on, Gameday lets you keep track of every MLB team as they play live. Game audio feeds can even be paused if you need to tear your attention from the game for a moment.

❯ Why we like it

This is pretty much a must-have for MLB fans. The information in the Gameday portion is invaluable for the armchair analyst, and the information is loaded quickly and includes cool animations. But our favorite part? No blackouts or restrictions on the audio feeds, a feature by itself that makes the price of this App worth it. It will have both teams' feeds of every game through the 2009 World Series. Best of all, it's live and well-synced with the Gameday features.

[
Interested in hearing a different point of view on the game you're listening to? Try switching to the opposing team's audio feed. It can be fun to hear a different perspective on your favorite team, and you can gain a lot of unique insight about the opponent.
]

quick review
★★★☆☆

Sports Radio

Developer: Intersect World, LLC ✦ **Genre:** Sports
Price: $0.99 ✦ **Release:** June 4, 2009

Summary

Featuring access to some of the most popular local sports radio stations, having the Sports Radio App means you'll never be caught out of market or miss out on the sports analysis you want to hear. Including the big local stations from nearly every major American city as well as national sports radio stations, Sports Radio has it all. The App supports dynamic editing of the server list, so if you want to add your favorite station to the list of available stations when they make their stream available, you can do it without having to update the App.

Why we like it

With a super easy-to-use interface, Sports Radio only has two main categories, National and Local, meaning you'll never get lost in the shuffle. With buttons for accessing the streams, favorites, and recently accessed stations, Sports Radio is simple and intuitive. The ability to mail links to friends or post them online is a neat feature that allows you to tune friends in when a station is discussing something of particular interest.

Sports

quick review
★★★☆☆

ESPN ScoreCenter

Developer: ESPN + **Genre:** Sports
Price: FREE + **Release:** May 28, 2009

> ### Summary

Ever need to look up a quick score
to see how your favorite team is doing? From
the Super Bowl to the French Open and every
sporting event in between, ESPN ScoreCenter
has the score. It's fast and easy to use, and
each game has its box score, key plays,
home runs, touchdowns, tries and wickets
available at the tap of a finger. Additionally,
ESPN's now-famous Bottom Line crawls
across the bottom of your screen to provide
breaking news updates from the world of
sports.

> ### Why we like it

If it's a sport, it's on here. ESPN ScoreCenter
treats every sport league like a "card" that can
be flipped over for more info. ESPN claims to
feature over 500 sports leagues in the App,
and that's certainly what it seems like: even
fans of sports not popular in America, like
rugby and cricket, will be more than happy
to see their sports represented. ESPN is not
resting on their laurels, either: they promise
to add more leagues and sports quickly, and
with the updates they have already made,
this seems to be happening already.

[
To stay current on any updates or leagues being added to ESPN
ScoreCenter, visit their Twitter page. The developers are also quick to
respond to suggestions or even answer questions about their App from
users. Look for a link to the page on the App's page in the App Store.
]

quick review
★★★☆☆

Sportacular

Developer: Citizen Sports, Inc. + **Genre:** Sports
Price: FREE + **Release:** March 7, 2009

Summary ‹

There's no need to switch from sport to sport when it comes to following your teams if you're using Sportacular. A sleek, easy to use sports score, news, and player tracker, Sportacular features every major North American sports league and every major European soccer league as well. Allowing users to track their favorite players and teams by creating custom lists for the App to follow, Sportacular allows you to see the information you want without having to sort through heaps of other scores. In addition to scores, statistics and schedules are easy to access with just a tap.

Why we like it ‹

While there are many sports score Apps out there, Sportacular is notable for its community aspects. While you're following your team in the App, Sportacular allows you to chat with your Facebook friends about the game or whatever else you feel like chatting about. Also, users can predict the winner and score of each game with other members of the Sportacular community, a fun way to participate in following the game and to see what others think about the potential outcome.

Sports

[Want to follow your fantasy teams and players without leaving the App? Create a custom list of players with the members of your teams and see all the stats update in real-time as your players compete, letting you stick with one App instead of tapping through several.]

quick review
★★★★☆

BreakMeter

Developer: Teego, LLC + **Genre:** Sports
Price: $0.99 + **Release:** July 29, 2008

❯ Summary

Looking to shave a few strokes off your golf score? Of course you are—every golfer would like to be just a little bit better. If you struggle with properly reading putts, then Break-Meter is the App for you. You no longer have to worry about gauging the break of a putt, as BreakMeter uses the accelerometer of your iPhone or iPod Touch to read the break in both left or right pitch, and uphill or downhill slope, when placed on the green.

❯ Why we like it

It helps take the guesswork out of putting! Knowing which way the green is sloping and the degree of that pitch helps any player to figure out which is the best angle to strike the ball. With new course designs becoming ever more challenging for average players, Break-Meter can become an invaluable tool for improving a putting game. Better putting is the easiest way for a player to shave strokes off their game, and the large golf ball and arrow on the screen leave no doubt when figuring out which way the break is going.

[alf you don't take your iPhone out on the course or your home course doesn't allow it, BreakMeter is still useful on the practice green or when putting at home. You can use it to learn how to properly visualize breaks and prepare for those clutch moments on the course.]

quick review
★★★☆☆

Fox Sports Mobile

Developer: Fox Sports Interactive + **Genre:** Sports
Price: FREE + **Release:** October 17, 2008

Summary

One of the most comprehensive sports Apps available, Fox Sports Mobile brings the power of Fox Sports to the iPhone and iPod Touch. With fantastic speed, scores, stats, and game recaps are available for every major sport including NASCAR race updates and full leader boards. Fox Sports Mobile sets itself apart from other sports Apps by including team pages and news stories, which can be read in the App without having to open a Safari page. Best of all, it's free!

Why we like it

A big plus comes in the form of the Fox Sports Video clips. The top five highlights of the day are ready to be accessed at any time, perfect for a quick glance at the top headlines of the sports day without having to turn on the TV. Another major reason to check out Fox Sports Mobile is the newly-added MLB Game-Trax: a great way to see what's going on in every MLB game. GameTrax allows users to see who's on base, at bat, pitching and on deck while also featuring in-depth box scores and game reports.

[NASCAR draws the largest crowds of any sport in North America, and only Fox Sports Mobile brings the thunder when it comes to the Sprint Cup. Each race page features a depiction of the track and information about the race in addition to the current race standings.]

Apps Capsules

● iScore Baseball Scorekeeper

Developer: Faster Than Monkeys ✦ **Genre:** Sport
Price: $4.99 ✦ **Release:** May 26, 2009

The easiest and most intuitive way to keep score of a baseball or softball game, iScore Baseball Scorekeeper lets you throw away that oldschool pencil (with eraser) and scorecard when you want to keep track of a game.

● ProCreative Golf 09

Developer: ProCreative, Inc. ✦ **Genre:** Sports
Price: $14.99 ✦ **Release:** June 14, 2009

Simple to use but packed with feature after feature, ProCreative Golf supports scorecard entry, photos from your round, GPS shot tracking, and handicap keeping. Keep track of your stats, e-mail your scores, and much more with ProCreative Golf.

● Golf Handicap Calculator

Developer: JoesApps ✦ **Genre:** Sports
Price: $1.99 ✦ **Release:** June 15, 2009

Ever wonder how you stack up against other golfers but don't have a country club membership? Use the Golf Handicap Calculator to gauge your skill level using USGA calculations.

● NFL—InGameNow

Developer: InGameNow ✦ **Genre:** Sports
Price: FREE ✦ **Release:** November 16, 2008

Featuring scores and news on every NFL game, NFL—InGameNow allows you to chat about the games with other fans. From friendly banter to deeper analysis, dig deeper with fellow fans and friends for a richer game-watching experience.

The Hockey News

Developer: Polar Mobile ✦ **Genre:** Sports
Price: FREE ✦ **Release:** March 30, 2009

Stay informed of all the latest scores and news
with The Hockey News App. Featuring the same
in-depth reporting and feature stories that dot the
monthly magazine, The Hockey News is a
must-have App for fans of cold steel on ice.

iScuba Plan Lite

Developer: Brock Brinkerhoff ✦ **Genre:** Sports
Price: FREE ✦ **Release:** April 26, 2009

A fast and accurate dive planner for recreational
Scuba divers, iScuba Plan allows you to get ready
for your next dive. Allowing for infinite variables
including the unknown "what ifs?" iScuba Plan is
detailed and easy to use.

CarTrack

Developer: Richard Shearman ✦ **Genre:** Sports
Price: $3.99 ✦ **Release:** March 2, 2009

Ever wonder just how well your car is performing?
Check out CarTrack for detailed information about
your vehicle's performance. It can tell you how fast
you're going, how hard you accelerate, and even
the g-forces you're experiencing.

Pointstreak K-ForCE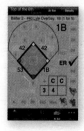

Developer: Pointstreak.com ✦ **Genre:** Sports
Price: $9.99 ✦ **Release:** May 23, 2009

Looking for a detailed scorekeeping software for
baseball and softball? Pointstreak's K-ForCE is
high-powered but still easy to use, allowing for
stats to be exported via e-mail and even to the
web for everyone to see.

Sports

quick review
★★★★★

Google Earth

Developer: Google + **Genre:** Travel
Price: FREE + **Release:** February 2, 2009

Summary

The mobile version of Google's immensely popular desktop software, Google Earth puts a whole new perspective on the world around us. With just a swipe of your finger, you can fly to all the corners of the globe, or just take a look down the street. Featuring the same stunning aerial and satellite imagery that made the desktop version such a big hit, Google Earth has high-resolution images for over half the world's population and over one-third of its land mass. Plus, Google Earth links up with other Google services to tell you even more about any location you choose.

Why we like it

In Chicago staring at the Sears Tower? Use Google Earth to quickly link you to the Wikipedia article about the building. Checking out the Coliseum in Rome? Google Earth has a link for that too. Google Local Search integrates seamlessly to provide information about attractions, restaurants, and other points of interest near your location. The App is available in 16 different languages, meaning just about everyone can have fun scouring the planet with Google Earth.

quick review
★★★☆☆

FlightTrack

Developer: Ben Kazez + **Genre:** Travel
Price: $4.99 + **Release:** April 26, 2009

Summary

Get real-time status updates for commercial flights from around the globe with the much-beloved FlightTrack. Whether you're about to fly or are waiting on the ground, you can view the progress of any flight you desire, including the map of its route. You can check what gate a flight is heading to, if it is delayed, or even if it's been cancelled. While a friend or loved one is in the air, use FlightTrack to see what plane they're on, how fast they're moving, and even what altitude they're at. Cool.

Why we like it

If you travel frequently or have a loved one who does, this App will quickly become a favorite. The FlightStats engine behind Flight-Track is used in major airports around the world to track their flights, so you're jacked into the same technology they use! If you're at the airport or need to forward flight information to someone, just tap an e-mail to them with the critical data. No subscription is needed for FlightTrack since your one-time fee will cover updates to the App and future additions to the flight database.

Are you a frequent flyer? Save your usual flights so they are auto-updated with FlightTrack. If you want more information such as airport closures, flight itineraries and weather forecasts for your departure and arrival cities, try upgrading to FlightTrack Pro.

Urbanspoon

Developer: Wanderspot, LLC + **Genre:** Travel
Price: FREE + **Release:** November 1, 2008

> Summary

Stuck in a new city and trying to find good dining options? Sitting at home and thinking about trying a new place to eat? A darling of early Apple TV commercials, Urbanspoon can help you decide what and where to eat. A cool, slot machine-like interface gorged with restaurant information, Urbanspoon will help you find a new spot with just a shake of your iPhone or iPod Touch. Using the built-in GPS technology, Urbanspoon can help you find the right place that's not too far away. It also supports international cities including London and several in Australia.

> Why we like it

This App is simple and direct. It won't overload you with information all at once—just shake and let it do its menu magic. As you shake, you can lock in any of the wheels, including price, location, and style of food to refine your next search's results. You can then share your results with friends to see if they have any suggestions for you. The community aspect is cool as well. You can post reviews and photos from the restaurants to Facebook for all your friends to see.

[Not sure whether to trust Urbanspoon's search results? They're backed up by links to reviews from bloggers, newspapers, and fellow Urbanspoon foodies. Save your favorite restaurants or just make a wish list of the places you want to try out. Mmmm good!]

quick review
★★★☆☆

Kayak

Developer: Kayak Software Corp. + **Genre:** Travel
Price: FREE + **Release:** February 11, 2009

Summary

There aren't many travel booking Apps in the App Store, but the big one that is there is Kayak. Possibly the most powerful travel search engine out there, Kayak will help you whether you have weeks to plan or need a flight that same day. You can book flights and hotel rooms online using their powerful search engine, or just tap a button to make a phone call and talk to a real person about your travel plans. Built-in hints help first-time users navigate Kayak's menus and make the right travel choices.

Why we like it

On the web, Kayak is possibly the most detailed and thorough flight booking site. In its App, Kayak brings all of this power into your hands, which is worth a recommendation in itself. Besides using its own engine to search for the best priced flights, Kayak allows users to search the other major travel websites for better deals, all with just one tap. The latest update has fixed many of the bugs plaguing the early releases of Kayak, making it more stable and faster to use than ever before.

[
For whatever reason, many travel websites don't yet have Apps available. Kayak covers for them by providing access to their search engines in addition to its own. When searching for flights and hotels, Kayak is smart about dates, figuring out when you're flying to choose the right dates for your hotel stay.
]

quick review
★★★★☆

HearPlanet

Developer: HearPlanet, Inc. + **Genre:** Travel
Price: $2.99 + **Release:** March 19, 2009

Summary

A talking tour guide for traveling through some of the world's coolest and most historic places, HearPlanet is like having a professional right next to you. With interactive maps and global coverage featuring over 250,000 sites, HearPlanet has something to say about nearly everywhere. It can use your iPhone or iPod Touch's GPS technology to help you find what's near you or what's going to be near where you're heading. New content is added daily, so search for your favorite places or head over to the Featured section of the App to see what's new.

Why we like it

For people who are intrigued by the sights and history around them, whether at home or on vacation, HearPlanet is as cool as it gets. You might just be amazed by what you find out about the world around you, including nature preserves, historic buildings, culturally significant neighborhoods, and landmarks. You can even fire up HearPlanet while at a sports game to learn more about the arena or stadium you're in. The interactive maps are extra layers of goodness on this wonderfully useful and educational App.

[HearPlanet is constantly upgrading with professionally recorded sound clips, meaning that the App is always expanding. The creators are totally open and responsive to suggestions, so check out HearPlanet's website for contact information.]

quick review
★★★☆☆

Zagat To Go '09

Developer: Handmark, Inc. ✦ **Genre:** Travel
Price: $9.99 ✦ **Release:** February 4, 2009

Summary

For the price of less than one of their restaurant guides, Zagat To Go '09 brings the power of 45 different Zagat dining guides to you iPhone or iPod touch. The feature-rich environment can help you choose the restaurant for any occasion, and impress your guests. With detailed reviews, information about the restaurant, and reservation booking on the fly, you'll quickly become the go-to restaurant guru among your family and friends. Nightlife, hotels and shopping are also covered in Zagat To Go, making it a one-stop shop for the best places to go.

Why we like it

Because Zagat is one of the most trusted names in restaurant reviews. Readers have dined with reliable guidance for more than 30 years, and finally having all of this information in one place is a technologoical and gastrological delight! Over 40,000 restaurant ratings and reviews are packed into this App, and it's no surprise that it's featured on iPhones and iPod Touches in every Apple Store. With the powerful Advanced Search functions and each city's Best Of lists, there's no shortage of yummy places to try and Zagat To Go will help you get there.

[Just because Zagat covers the best restaurants an area has to offer, don't think all their suggestions are going to break the bank! Remember that "best" does not mean "most expensive," because there are many budget-conscious choices in Zagat's list of restaurants, including burger and pizza joints.]

Apps Capsules

> Yelp

Developer: Yelp, Inc. + **Genre:** Travel
Price: FREE + **Release:** September 15, 2008

Looking for a new hotspot near you? A late-night burrito place? A swanky dance club? Use your iPhone or iPod Touch's location finder and Yelp to locate just the place you're looking for near you.

> Trapster

Developer: Trapster.com + **Genre:** Travel
Price: FREE + **Release:** May 10, 2009

A high-tech way to let you know when you're approaching a speed trap or red light camera, Trapster keeps you informed of potential pratfalls on your drive. It also helps by reporting local traffic jams.

> Currency

Developer: Jeffrey Grossman + **Genre:** Travel
Price: FREE + **Release:** September 12, 2008

Providing up-to-date currency exchange information for 90 currencies used in over 100 countries, Currency is great for the traveler in a foreign country or the currency trader at home. Never get caught without knowing the current exchange rate.

> Tipulator

Developer: Sophia Teutschler + **Genre:** Travel
Price: $1.99 + **Release:** March 18, 20099

The quick and easy way to calculate your tip at a restaurant, Tipulator does the hard work for you. Just tap in the bill amount and what percentage you want to tip.

myLanguage Translator

Developer: myLanguage, Inc. ✦ **Genre:** Travel
Price: FREE ✦ **Release:** March 10, 2009

Featuring support for dozens of languages with
more added all the time, myLanguage Translator is
a powerful translation tool. Best of all, it has entry
in landscape mode.

Cheap Gas!

Developer: David J. Hinson ✦ **Genre:** Travel
Price: FREE ✦ **Release:** September 9, 2008

Want to save money on gas? Pick up Cheap Gas
today to help you find the cheapest gasoline in your
area. Cheap Gas shows you the station, the prices
for all grades, and how far the station is from you.

Taxi

Developer: Applandia ✦ **Genre:** Travel
Price: FREE ✦ **Release:** August 17, 2008

Frustrated by not being able to hail a cab where you
are or just want a taxi to come pick you up? Download Taxi and summon a cab with a single tap.

LiveATC Air Radio

Developer: LiveATC.net ✦ **Genre:** Travel
Price: $2.99 ✦ **Release:** May 25, 2009

Stuck at the airport or on your way and wondering
what's going on in the cockpits or in Air Traffic
Control? Listen in live with LiveATC at over 250
airports worldwide.

Travel

quick review
★★★☆☆

AT&T myWireless Mobile

Developer: AT&T, Inc. + **Genre:** Utilities
Price: FREE + **Release:** May 1, 2009

> Summary

An App straight from your wireless provider, AT&T myWireless Mobile brings such functionality to your iPhone that you may never look at that confusing paper bill in the mail again. If you've already registered for online account management with AT&T Mobility, you're good to go. If you're not already registered, it just takes a few minutes to sign up. You can instantly log in and pay your bill directly from your iPhone, add or remove features, or even see how many minutes or text messages you have left in the month.

> Why we like it

Not only is the interface intuitive and elegantly designed, the features are rich and useful for anyone who does not like to sort through a paper bill each month. Everything about your bill including full, detailed usage information is there. This App should be included right out of the box as it is so useful for users. Since everyone that has an iPhone in the U.S. is on the AT&T network at this time, we recommend this as a must-add for everyone.

[Want to add features to your plan like unlimited text messaging or early nights and weekend rates? There's no need to call a customer service representative any more, as you can make changes to your service within the App.]

quick review
★★★★☆

iHandy Carpenter

Developer: iHandySoft, Inc. **+ Genre:** Utilities
Price: $1.99 **+ Release:** April 23, 2009

Summary

If you do anything around the house that involves wood work or hanging stuff on walls, you need the tools of iHandy Carpenter. With two kinds of levels, a plumb bob, protractor, and a ruler, you'll find yourself using this App all the time. From hanging pictures to drawing a template, iHandy Carpenter will save you time and give you accurate measurements. Beautifully designed and fully-featured, this App is a great solution for anyone who has a need for this type of functionality and flexibility. And frankly, who doesn't?

Why we like it

The graphics of the tools look good and each tool is easy to use and is noticeably effective. The levels and plumb bob can help you make accurate adjustments by displaying precise angles (as long as your device is calibrated properly.) If you're doing simple work around the house or workshop you can eliminate the need to bring out some of your oldschool tools.

[Not sure how long of a ruler you need? Don't worry, the ruler in this App is endless! Just keep swiping the screen and the ruler can go on forever. The iHandy Carpenter App is a great value, since the individual tools cost one dollar each.]

9-Toolbox

Developer: e2ndesign **+ Genre:** Utilities
Price: FREE **+ Release:** May 18, 2009

> Summary

Free for a limited time, 9-Toolbox (despite its name) crams 15 often-used features under the umbrella of one App. Doing nothing unique but simply bringing things like a flashlight, unit converter, holiday calendar and loan calculator under one roof, 9-Toolbox will quickly replace other Apps on your iPhone or iPod touch thanks to its great utility. These Apps aren't watered down either: the holiday calendar includes 83 countries, the currency converter has 164 different monies and the inclinometer has three different units it's able to display.

> Why we like it

Instead of having to download a special App for a feature that you don't need often, it's nice to have a toolbox of common Apps that you can access regularly. With space limitations on how many Apps you can load, 9-Toolbox is a great way to eliminate some individual Apps you may not use much. The developers have made an effort to unify the design of each tool in the App and make it seamless to switch between utilities. New tools are being added, so watch out for updates.

[Even at the App's original price of $4.99, there was still a great deal of value in 9-Toolbox. The units conversion is accurate, the tip calculator is useful every time you go out for a meal—hardly a day will go by that you don't find a use for one of the tools.]

quick review
★★★☆☆

Units

Developer: TheMacBox **+ Genre:** Utilities
Price: FREE **+ Release:** July 1, 2008

Summary

If you have a need to convert measurements
for any reason, Units is the App for you.
Whether it's for school, work, or to settle a
discussion among friends, Units is free, fast,
and has hundreds of different calculations built
in. With categories as wide-ranging as Area,
Currency, Time, Weight and Speed, just about
anything that has multiple measures is covered
in Units. It can handle metric to Imperial and
back again, plus other methods of calculation
including Kelvin for temperature, among
others. If you need it converted, Units is your
all-purpose solution.

Why we like it

There are so many different conversions available in Units that it would take a very difficult
or complicated conversion to be beyond the
scope of the App. Never having to know the
conversion factor is nice—there are so many
different multipliers that it's all too easy to
make a mistake. Units removes this variable
with an easy-to-use interface that makes sure
you select the right measure every time. The
App even includes a built-in ruler to allow you
measure shorter objects in a pinch.

After units of physical measure, currency conversion is probably the
function you will use most. Units recognizes that this is a popular
conversion and adds the abstract science of currency to the App.
Though the exchange rates are not as up-to-date as more specialized
Apps, it's a thoughtful feature.

Apps Capsules

◉ A Fake Caller

Developer: Hot Potato ✦ **Genre:** Utilities
Price: FREE ✦ **Release:** April 27, 2009

Need to get out of a boring date or meeting but
have no way to tactfully exit the room? Fire up
A Fake Caller to fake a call from someone in
your contacts list. Gotta go!

◉ Speedtest.net Speed Test

Developer: Ookla ✦ **Genre:** Utilities
Price: FREE ✦ **Release:** December 19, 2008

Measure your network speed with the most trusted
names in the business, Speedtest.net. Use their
massive global network to test the speed of your
connection against others in your area or on your ISP.

◉ Have2Eat

Developer: AT&T Interactive R&D ✦ **Genre:** Utilities
Price: FREE ✦ **Release:** March 24, 2009

Have2Eat displays restaurant information for your
current area or any place you want to search. Your
results have a simple thumbs up or thumbs down
rating to know if others like the place or not.

◉ LCube Lite

Developer: CoolMoon Corp ✦ **Genre:** Utilities
Price: FREE ✦ **Release:** May 26, 2009

Inspired by the popular puzzle of the 1980, LCube
Lite will test your mind and patience. You can also
input any combination of colors on your own and
even watch LCube Lite solve the puzzle for you.

Most Wanted

Developer: NICUSA + **Genre:** Utilities
Price: FREE + **Release:** May 30, 2009

Get a handle on the Top Ten Most Wanted, missing children, and wanted terrorists with Most Wanted. The App provides background info and pictures about each person on the lists with a link to send information to the FBI.

MultiConvert

Developer: Kreative Software + **Genre:** Utilities
Price: FREE + **Release:** December 12, 2008

Featuring over 1,000 units in 50 categories, MultiConvert is the most flexible conversion App available. Use list mode, try out the built-in calculator, or just watch your units update in real time.

Spell Check

Developer: Achoom + **Genre:** Utilities
Price: FREE + **Release:** February 25, 2009

A simple and yet very useful App, Spell Check is both a spell checker and full-featured dictionary. Requiring no internet connection, Spell Check helps you correct your documents or find a word you were trying to spell correctly.

Planets

Developer: Q Continuum + **Genre:** Utilities
Price: FREE + **Release:** February 17, 2009

Locate your favorite planets and stars in the tonight's sky with Planets. Uncover the locations of the celestial objects and find out when the moon and planets rise and set.

Utilities

quick review
★★★★★

The Weather Channel

Developer: The Weather Channel + **Genre:** Weather
Price: FREE + **Release:** November 4, 2008

› Summary

The big boy of the weather reporting world, The Weather Channel was quick to join the App Store from the get-go. Though Apple's built-in App is fine for a quick check of weather, The Weather Channel takes it several steps further with live radar, dynamic forecasts that include video for national and international locations, and multiple location storage. If you live in a major metropolitan area, you'll also be thankful for the traffic cams that give you a real-time look at road conditions.

› Why we like it

The Weather Channel utilizes the location awareness capabilities of the iPhone and iPod Touch seamlessly, providing the local weather at just the touch of a button. We especially like the Severe Weather button in the App, allowing you to see where it is getting nasty wherever you are, a very useful feature on road trips. Also, if you're meeting with a friend or just need to let someone else know how the weather is in whatever place you choose, you can e-mail a weather report right to them.

quick review
★★★★☆

The Snow Report

Developer: The North Face **+ Genre:** Weather
Price: FREE **+ Release:** November 20, 2008

Summary

A must for any snow sports enthusiast, The Snow Report will quickly become an essential tool for hitting the slopes. Offering detailed snow reports for any resort and detailed weather reports from NOAA for U.S. resorts, The Snow Report will tell you everything there is to know about the conditions on the mountain. It will tell you the base layer, snow condition, expected snowfall, and even provide a link to the mountain's website. Best of all, The Snow Report also packs in information for resorts from around the world.

Why we like it

One of the best features of The Snow Report is Trail Maps. At a resort with many intersecting runs or simply a resort like Jackson Hole with 120 marked trails, it can be easy to become lost or disoriented and end up going down a run that may be too easy, too hard, or end at the wrong lift. Never again with the dynamic trail maps! Plan your route down the mountain while going up the lift and zoom in on trouble spots to make sure your skis are always heading down the right hill.

This App is well-rounded and is perhaps the only ski report App to offer detailed snow information about every major resort. It can help you decide which mountain to ski, which coat to put on and which run to take, making it an incredibly practical App.

Weather

Apps Capsules

◉ WeatherBug Elite

Developer: AWS Convergence Technologies, Inc.
Genre: Weather + **Price:** $0.99
Release: March 30, 2009

Getting the paid version of the popular WeatherBug App, $0.99 will net you an ad-free, constantly up-graded App. Featuring real-time radar and forecasts, WeatherBug Elite is an easy-to-use and powerful App.

◉ Weather Radio

Developer: Marco Papa + **Genre:** Weather
Price: $0.99 + **Release:** May 19, 2009

Providing access to official NOAA weather stations, Weather Radio is a one stop shop for weather reports. Also providing emergency alerts from NOAA covering the United States, Weather Radio gets you the right information wherever you are.

◉ Who is Hot?

Developer: Weather Underground + **Genre:** Weather
Price: FREE + **Release:** July 2, 2008

Instantly check the weather wherever your contacts are to find out who's sitting in the sun and who's staying inside out of the rain. Your current location is found using GPS, which also makes the App a digital thermometer.

◉ FlashBang

Developer: Refactr, LLC + **Genre:** Weather
Price: FREE + **Release:** March 6, 2009

Cue up FlashBang to figure out how near that storm really is. Hit "Lightning" when you see the strike and press "Thunder" when you hear it to find out exactly how far you are from a strike.

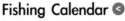

Fishing Calendar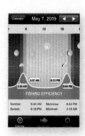

Developer: SIS Software ✦ **Genre:** Weather
Price: $3.99 ✦ **Release:** April 18, 2009

The perfect App for the avid fisherman, Fishing Calendar helps to plan out your fishing trip by using information on the weather, tides, sun and moon to calculate the best times to drop a line in the water.

SnoCountry Free

Developer: Seven2, Inc. ✦ **Genre:** Weather
Price: FREE ✦ **Release:** March 26, 2009

Selecting from a list of favorite resorts, SnoCountry lets users look at the snow report for their favorite mountains while providing buttons to call the resorts or even view their webcams.

Hurricane

Developer: Kitty Code, LLC ✦ **Genre:** Weather
Price: $3.99 ✦ **Release:** January 28, 2009

The award-winning Hurricane is a must-have for people who live in or are travelling to places where storms may affect them. Offering real-time tracking and storm data, Hurricane also provides text alerts that constantly update a storm's direction.

Sunrise Sunset

Developer: Kokoa Vincent ✦ **Genre:** Weather
Price: $0.99 ✦ **Release:** March 20, 2009

A simple and easy to use App that benefits folks like photographers and golfers, Sunrise Sunset provides accurate and detailed information about lunar and solar cycles using either GPS or a large list of stored cities.

Weather

Index